HOPE 1:8

MISSIONS CO-OP

THE ACTS OF TEXAS BAPTISTS

The book of Acts is the story of the church's advancement to the ends of the earth through the power of the Holy Spirit. The theme of the book is the expansion of the Kingdom of God on earth. It's this truth that sets the direction for the church as a body of believers and sets the direction for a convention of churches working together, the BGCT.

In Acts, we as believers become known as Christians, and the book discusses the conflicts and changes that happened in society as a result of God's Kingdom message going from place to place and from people to people. Jesus challenged the established society and its understanding of faith and action. His early followers did the same. We as today's representatives of Jesus Christ should continue their example.

"But you will receive power when the Holy Spirit comes on you; and you will be my witnesses in Jerusalem, and in all of Judea and Samaria, and to the ends of the earth."

Acts 1:8

"But you will receive power when the Holy Spirit comes on you; and you will be my witnesses in Jerusalem, and in all of Judea and Samaria, and to the ends of the earth." Acts 1:8 is about empowering and challenging us to be His witnesses where we are and where we go. In essence, to always be on mission.

Hope 1:8 is a Texas Baptist emphasis that is based on this scripture and mandate to constantly be on mission to reach your neighbors, state, nation and world for Christ. One of the beautiful aspects in Acts 1:8 is the fact that we are not sent out alone, but with the Holy Spirit to guide our thoughts, words and actions to better be His witness that His message of hope may be heard.

Hope 1:8 isn't a program or set of actions to take, but rather a focus on enabling you and your church to be personally involved in mission trips – across the street or across the world. It concentrates on cooperative missions that reach the world beyond our typical circle of influence. Our neighbors, cities, state, nation and world are waiting for us to take action.

We were created for fellowship with God. Through that relationship, God is calling us to Christian worship and service through the church He established. Your church is also the hub through which Christ's love will permeate society and change people's lives. Hope 1:8 exists to energize you and your church to organize in mission action, mission education and mission funding as a body of believers.

" I welcome each of you to join your church and your BGCT in Hope 1:8 by giving to missions, being on mission, and praying for lives to be impacted and God's message to be heard. **"**

— Dr. David Hardage

To assist in local, national and international mission trips, there are two Texas Baptist resources available to you. First is BeOnMission.org, an online, interactive missions finder tool that is searchable by location, type of mission work and duration. The other is Texas Partnerships, a Texas Baptists ministry office that connects churches and institutions to specific projects with sister Baptist churches and conventions in the U.S. and around the globe. Texas Partnerships will also help prepare your mission team with training, orientation and several of the logistics of international travel.

TEXAS ★ BAPTISTS

BAPTIST GENERAL CONVENTION OF TEXAS

333 N. Washington | Dallas, TX 75246-1798 | 888.244.9400 | www.texasbaptists.org

BE ON
MISSION

Be On Mission is a unique online missions locator tool that connects individuals and churches with missions opportunities locally and around the world. It also tracks missions opportunities through stories, blog posts, photos and video. The vision for Be On Mission is to provide a missions experience for the group in the field, as well as for those who are at home, motivating them to pursue the ultimate goal of spreading the gospel. Join us in our efforts to spread the gospel by committing to be on mission.

TEXAS ★ BAPTISTS

BAPTIST GENERAL CONVENTION OF TEXAS

texasbaptists.org/beonmission

BAPTISTWAY ADULT BIBLE STUDY GUIDE®

The Book of Acts

TIME TO ACT ON ACTS 1:8

DUANE BROOKS · RANDEL EVERETT · BRIAN HARBOUR
PHIL LINEBERGER · JOHN OGLETREE · ELLIS OROZCO
JESSE RINCONES · WESLEY SHOTWELL
BYRON STEVENSON · ROSS WEST · DENNIS WILES
SANDY WISDOM-MARTIN · JULIE WOOD

BAPTISTWAYPRESS®
Dallas, Texas

BAPTISTWAY PRESS® Leadership Team
Executive Director, Baptist General Convention of Texas: David Hardage
Director, Education/Discipleship Center: Chris Liebrum
Director, Bible Study/Discipleship Team: Phil Miller

Publishing consultant and editor: Ross West
Cover and Interior Design and Production: Desktop Miracles, Inc.
Printing: Data Reproductions Corporation

First edition: September 2012

ISBN-13: 978-1-934731-93-2

How to Make the Best Use of This Issue

Whether you're the teacher or a student—

1. Start early in the week before your class meets.

2. Overview the study. Review the table of contents and read the study introduction. Try to see how each lesson relates to the overall study.

3. Use your Bible to read and consider prayerfully the Scripture passages for the lesson. (You'll see that each writer has chosen a favorite translation for the lessons in this issue. You're free to use the Bible translation you prefer and compare it with the translation chosen for that unit, of course.)

4. After reading all the Scripture passages in your Bible, then read the writer's comments. The comments are intended to be an aid to your study of the Bible.

5. Read the small articles—"sidebars"—in each lesson. They are intended to provide additional, enrichment information and inspiration and to encourage thought and application.

6. Try to answer for yourself the questions included in each lesson. They're intended to encourage further thought and application, and they can also be used in the class session itself.

If you're the teacher—

A. Do all of the things just mentioned, of course. As you begin the study with your class, be sure to find a way to help your class know the date on which each lesson will be studied. You might do this in one or more of the following ways:

  • In the first session of the study, briefly overview the study by identifying with your class the date on which each lesson will be studied. Lead your class to write the date in the table of contents on page 11 and on the first page of each lesson.

- Make and post a chart that indicates the date on which each lesson will be studied.
- If all of your class has e-mail, send them an e-mail with the dates the lessons will be studied.
- Provide a bookmark with the lesson dates. You may want to include information about your church and then use the bookmark as an outreach tool, too. A model for a bookmark can be downloaded from www.baptistwaypress.org on the Resources for Adults page.
- Develop a sticker with the lesson dates, and place it on the table of contents or on the back cover.

B. Get a copy of the *Teaching Guide,* a companion piece to this *Study Guide.* The *Teaching Guide* contains additional Bible comments plus two teaching plans. The teaching plans in the *Teaching Guide* are intended to provide practical, easy-to-use teaching suggestions that will work in your class.

C. After you've studied the Bible passage, the lesson comments, and other material, use the teaching suggestions in the *Teaching Guide* to help you develop your plan for leading your class in studying each lesson.

D. Teaching resource items for use as handouts are available free at www.baptistwaypress.org.

E. You may want to get the additional adult Bible study comments— *Adult Online Bible Commentary*—by Dr. Jim Denison (president, Denison Forum on Truth and Culture, and theologian-in-residence, Baptist General Convention of Texas). Call 1–866–249–1799 or e-mail baptistway@texasbaptists.org to order *Adult Online Bible Commentary.* It is available only in electronic format (PDF) from our website, www.baptistwaypress.org. The price of these comments is $6 for individuals and $25 for a group of five. A church or class that participates in our advance order program for free shipping can receive *Adult Online Bible Commentary* free. Call 1–866–249–1799 or see www.baptistwaypress.org to purchase or for information on participating in free shipping program for the next study.

F. Additional teaching plans are also available in electronic format (PDF) by calling 1–866–249–1799. The price of these additional teaching plans is $5 for an individual and $20 for a group of five. A church or class that participates in our advance order program for free shipping can receive *Adult Online Teaching Plans* free. Call 1–866–249–1799 or see www.baptistwaypress.org for information on participating in our free shipping program for the next study.

G. You also may want to get the enrichment teaching help that is provided on the internet by the *Baptist Standard* at www.baptiststandard.com. (Other class participants may find this information helpful, too.) Call 214–630–4571 to begin your subscription to the printed or electronic edition of the *Baptist Standard*.

H. Enjoy leading your class in discovering the meaning of the Scripture passages and in applying these passages to their lives.

DO YOU USE A KINDLE?

This BaptistWay *Adult Bible Study Guide* plus *Living Generously for Jesus' Sake; Profiles in Character; Amos, Hosea, Isaiah, Micah; The Gospel of Matthew; The Gospel of John: Part One; The Gospel of John: Part Two;* and *The Corinthian Letters: Imperatives for an Imperfect Church* are now available in a Kindle edition. The easiest way to find these materials is to search for "BaptistWay" on your Kindle or go to www.amazon.com/kindle and do a search for "BaptistWay." The Kindle edition can be studied not only on a Kindle but also on a PC, Mac, iPhone, iPad, Blackberry, or Android phone using the Kindle app available free from amazon.com/kindle.

Audio Bible Study Lessons

Do you want to use your walk/run/ride, etc. time to study the Bible? Or maybe you're a college student who wants to listen to the lesson on your iPod®? Or maybe you're looking for a way to study the Bible when you just can't find time to read? Or maybe you know someone who has difficulty seeing to read even our *Large Print Study Guide*?

Then try our audio Bible study lessons, available on this study plus *Living Generously for Jesus' Sake; Profiles in Character; Amos, Hosea, Isaiah, Micah; The Gospel of Matthew; The Gospel of Luke; The Gospel of John: Part One; The Gospel of John: Part Two; The Corinthian Letters; Galatians and 1 & 2 Thessalonians;* and *The Letters of James and John.* For more information or to order, call 1–866–249–1799 or e-mail baptistway@texasbaptists.org. The files are downloaded from our website. You'll need an audio player that plays MP3 files (like an iPod®, but many MP3 players are available), or you can listen on a computer.

Writers of This Study Guide

Randel Everett, pastor of First Baptist Church of Midland, Texas, wrote **lesson one.** Dr. Everett previously served as executive director of the Baptist General Convention of Texas and as pastor in Texas, Arkansas, Florida, and Virginia. He served also as founding president of the John Leland Center for Theological Studies.

Jesse Rincones, pastor of Alliance Church in Lubbock, Texas, wrote **lesson two.** Jesse earned a degree in mathematics from Texas Tech University and also a Juris Doctor degree. He serves as president of the Hispanic Baptist Convention of Texas and trustee for the Baptist University of the Americas.

Julie (Brown) Wood wrote **lesson three.** She is a graduate of Hardin-Simmons University and Southwestern Baptist Theological Seminary. She is a member of Central Baptist Church, Jacksonville, Texas. A former children's minister and worship leader, she now serves as a freelance writer and as pianist for Jacksonville Independent School District choirs.

John Ogletree, Jr., writer of **lesson four,** is senior pastor and founder of First Metropolitan Baptist Church, Houston, Texas. He earned his bachelor's degree from the University of Texas at Arlington and his Doctor of Jurisprudence degree from South Texas College of Law, Houston. He has served on the Executive Board of the Baptist General Convention of Texas and also as president of the African-American Fellowship Association of BGCT.

Sandy Wisdom-Martin wrote **lesson five.** Sandy is the executive director-treasurer for Woman's Missionary Union (WMU) of Texas. She served in the areas of WMU and Church and Community Ministries with the Arkansas Baptist State Convention for ten years, and then she served with the Illinois Baptist State Association for nearly ten years in a similar capacity.

Duane Brooks, writer of **lesson six,** is pastor, Tallowood Baptist Church, Houston, Texas. Dr. Brooks has served on the Executive Board and the Human Welfare Board of the Baptist General Convention of Texas and on the Board of Regents at Baylor University. He holds the Ph.D. from Baylor University.

Wesley Shotwell, writer of **lesson seven,** is pastor of Ash Creek Baptist Church, Azle, Texas. Dr. Shotwell formerly was pastor of churches in Tennessee. He is a graduate of Baylor University (B.A.), Southwestern Baptist Theological Seminary (M.Div.), and Vanderbilt Divinity School (D.Min.).

Byron Stevenson wrote **lesson eight.** He is senior pastor of The Fort Bend Church in Sugar Land, Texas. He is a graduate of Southern University, Baton Rouge, Louisiana, with a Bachelor of Science in Accounting, and he also earned a Masters of Arts in Theological Studies degree from Houston Baptist University. He was elected as second vice president of the Baptist General Convention of Texas in 2011.

Ross West wrote **lesson nine.** He assisted in beginning BaptistWay Press and then served as publisher. He has served churches in Kentucky, Arkansas, Virginia, Louisiana, and Georgia as pastor or associate pastor, and he also has served as an editorial section manager at the Baptist Sunday School Board, Nashville, Tennessee. He is a graduate of Louisiana Tech University, The Southern Baptist Theological Seminary, and New Orleans Baptist Theological Seminary.

Dennis Wiles, writer of **lesson ten,** serves as pastor of First Baptist Church of Arlington, Texas. Along with his wife, Cindy, they have established Kinexxus, a church-based network designed to encourage and train local churches in collaborating for the accomplishment of the mission of God. First Baptist Arlington is the primary supporter of Mission Arlington, a local church-based community ministry. The church also is training and sending workers across the world in response to God's leadership.

Brian Harbour wrote **lesson eleven.** After serving as a pastor for forty-two years, Dr. Harbour retired to give his attention to writing and teaching. He is president of SeminaryPLUS, a non-profit organization that provides coaching and encouragement to pastors. He also serves as an adjunct professor at Dallas Baptist University and as Visiting Professor in Religion at Baylor University.

Phil Lineberger, writer of **lesson twelve,** is pastor of Sugar Land Baptist Church, Sugar Land, Texas (formerly known as Williams Trace Baptist Church). He has served as president of the Baptist General Convention of Texas, as a trustee for William Jewell College and Dallas Baptist University, as a regent at Baylor University, and as vice-president of the Cotton Bowl Athletic Association.

Ellis Orozco wrote **lesson thirteen.** Dr. Orozco is pastor of First Baptist Church, Richardson, Texas. He graduated from Texas A&M with a degree in engineering and then earned his Master of Divinity from Southwestern Seminary and his Doctor of Ministry from Truett Seminary of Baylor University. He has served the Baptist General Convention of Texas in numerous ways.

The Book of Acts: Time to Act on Acts 1:8

Introducing

THE BOOK OF ACTS:
Time to Act on Acts 1:8

Acts 1:8—Our Challenge

Acts 1:8 serves as the touchstone for all of the Book of Acts, and it continues to challenge us today with our responsibilities to our Lord. Jesus communicated clearly and simply the challenge to those first disciples gathered about him, "But you will receive power when the Holy Spirit has come upon you; and you will be my witnesses in Jerusalem, in all Judea and Samaria, and to the ends of the earth" (Acts 1:8).[1]

The disciples often seemed to be out of touch with Jesus' identity and purpose, no matter how much time Jesus spent with them or how magnificent the experiences Jesus provided them. The resurrected Jesus had been with them forty days, "speaking about the kingdom of God" (1:3). Still they came to Jesus with a question out of their own agenda that showed their lack of understanding. They asked, "Lord, is this the time when you will restore the kingdom to Israel?" (1:6).

Jesus brushed aside their question, stating that such a question in essence was beyond their need to know, certainly one to which they did not need to give their attention. What they did need to know, though, was what their lives as Jesus' disciples were to be like as they served him. They needed to know that they were to be Jesus' witnesses and that they were to be Jesus' witnesses in areas with which they were familiar and comfortable and in areas with which they were not. They were to be

Jesus' "witnesses in Jerusalem, in all Judea and Samaria, and to the ends of the earth." Jesus' earliest followers would spend the rest of the Book of Acts learning and acting on what this statement meant. We're still learning—or should be.

Jesus' words are simply in the form of a statement—being Jesus' witnesses is what Jesus' disciples do. Even so, our failure in general to rise to the level of Jesus' words and accept our own responsibility to be Jesus' witnesses means that they come to us in the form of a challenge. Whatever agenda we and our church think is important, the clear statement from Jesus is that we are to be Jesus' witnesses. Indeed, we are to be Jesus' witnesses in our own Jerusalem, our own Judea, our own Samaria, our own "ends of the earth."

As with the church in the Book of Acts, we are to be Jesus' witnesses

- In our familiar surroundings—our Jerusalem
- In nearby places and opportunities—our Judea
- To the places, peoples, and cultures with which we feel much less comfortable and for which we must cross cultural barriers to witness and minister—our Samaria
- In the distant places that call for significant decisions for *us* to go or for significant support of others as *they* go to "the remotest part of the earth"

This Study

This study of the Book of Acts focus on thirteen portraits or vignettes of what being Jesus' witnesses meant in the lives of the early disciples. Many passages could have been chosen, of course. The passages chosen offer challenging guidance about what individuals and churches need to do to live up more closely to Jesus' statement in our day.

It's highly unlikely we have already done everything Jesus said we are supposed to do about Acts 1:8. Most likely we need openness to the Spirit's leading to show us where we are reluctant to be Jesus' witnesses; we need willingness to rely on the Spirit's power; and we need simply to get up and do what our Lord said we are to do. It is indeed *time to act on Acts 1:8.*

THE BOOK OF ACTS: TIME TO ACT ON ACTS 1:8

Additional Resources for Studying the Book of Acts[2]

F. F. Bruce. *The Book of the Acts.* The New International Commentary on the New Testament. Grand Rapids, Michigan: Eerdmans, 1988.

David Garland, New Testament editor. *Luke—Acts.* The Expositor's Bible Commentary. Volume 10. Revised edition. Grand Rapids, Michigan: Zondervan, 2007.

Richard N. Longenecker. "Acts." *The Expositor's Bible Commentary.* Grand Rapids, Michigan: Zondervan, 1981.

J. W. MacGorman. *Acts: The Gospel for All People.* Nashville, Tennessee: Convention Press, 1990.

Howard Marshall. *Acts.* Tyndale New Testament Commentaries. Grand Rapids, Michigan: Eerdmans, 1980.

John B. Polhill. *Acts.* The New American Commentary. Volume 26. Nashville, Tennessee: Broadman Press, 1992.

A. T. Robertson. *Word Pictures in the New Testament.* Volume III. Nashville, Tennessee: Broadman Press, 1930.

T.C. Smith. *Acts.* The Broadman Bible Commentary. Volume 10. Nashville, Tennessee: Broadman Press, 1970.

Frank Stagg. *The Book of Acts: The Early Struggle for an Unhindered Gospel.* Nashville, Tennessee: Broadman Press, 1955.

John R. W. Stott. *The Message of Acts.* The Bible Speaks Today. Downers Grove, Illinois: InterVarsity, 1994.

William H. Willimon. *Acts.* Interpretation: A Bible Commentary for Teaching and Preaching. Atlanta: John Knox Press, 1988.

NOTES

1. Unless otherwise indicated, all Scripture quotations in "Introducing the Book of Acts: Time to Act on Acts 1:8" and lessons 5 and 9 are taken from the New Revised Standard Version.

2. Listing a book does not imply full agreement by the writers or BAPTISTWAY PRESS® with all of its comments.

FOCAL TEXT
Acts 1:1–8

BACKGROUND
Acts 1:1–11

MAIN IDEA
Jesus instructed his
disciples that they were
to be his witnesses.

QUESTION TO EXPLORE
Whose witness are you?

STUDY AIM
To commit myself to be Jesus'
witness and to identify in
this series of Bible studies
how I will do that

QUICK READ
The apostles were confused
about the kingdom of God
even after Jesus' resurrection.
Jesus instructed them to
wait in Jerusalem until the
Holy Spirit empowered
them to be his witnesses.

LESSON ONE

Accept Responsibility for Being Jesus' Witness

The Book of Acts provides a compelling picture of the Holy Spirit moving among the early church as Christ is proclaimed throughout the world. Yet this book is much more than an historical document. God challenges the church of every age with the promise of Acts 1:8. We are to be Jesus' witnesses in Jerusalem, Judea, Samaria, and to the farthest reaches of the world.

Are you ready to accept your kingdom assignment?

ACTS 1:1–8

¹ The first account I composed, Theophilus, about all that Jesus began to do and teach, ² until the day when He was taken up to heaven, after He had by the Holy Spirit given orders to the apostles whom He had chosen. ³ To these He also presented Himself alive after His suffering, by many convincing proofs, appearing to them over a period of forty days and speaking of the things concerning the kingdom of God. ⁴ Gathering them together, He commanded them not to leave Jerusalem, but to wait for what the Father had promised, "Which," He said, "you heard of from Me; ⁵ for John baptized with water, but you will be baptized with the Holy Spirit not many days from now." ⁶ So when they had come together, they were asking Him, saying, "Lord, is it at this time You are restoring the kingdom to Israel?" ⁷ He said to them, "It is not for you to know times or epochs which the Father has fixed by His own authority; ⁸ but you will receive power when the Holy Spirit has come upon you; and you shall be My witnesses both in Jerusalem, and in all Judea and Samaria, and even to the remotest part of the earth."

Prologue to Acts (1:1–5)

Who is the writer? The Book of Acts does not directly identify its writer, but various strong clues within Acts indicate its human author was Luke, who also wrote the Gospel of Luke. Both Luke 1:3 and Acts 1:1 refer to Theophilus, and Acts 1:1 speaks of "the first account I composed."[1] Luke and Acts also have similarities in their style of language. In addition, the "we" passages in Acts suggest that the author was a traveling companion of Paul (Acts 16:10–17; 20:5–15; 21:1–8; 27:1—28:16). In Colossians 4:14, Luke is identified as "the doctor" and as being with Paul. Furthermore, church tradition beginning in the second century identified Luke as the author of Acts.[2]

Luke did not claim to be an eyewitness of the events of the gospel, and yet he obviously heard the testimony of those who were eyewitnesses. In Acts 1 Luke continued the story he began in the Gospel of Luke. Acts 1:1–11 restates much of what was written in Luke 24:44–53. The emphasis in both texts is that after Christ's ascension his followers would receive power and would be his witnesses to all the nations beginning in Jerusalem.

What is the occasion? After Jesus' resurrection, he met with the disciples showing many convincing proofs over a period of forty days. In 1 Corinthians 15:5–8, the Apostle Paul listed some of those who experienced Jesus' ministry after the resurrection.

As Jesus met with the disciples, he continued the message he preached before the crucifixion "concerning the kingdom of God" (Acts 1:3). The kingdom of God is not just an earthly fulfillment but an eternal reality that includes God's covenant with Israel and the church but is the reign of God forever.

It was obvious in verse 6 that the disciples were still looking for the restoration of Israel that would bring freedom from subjugation by the Romans. Jesus let them know that he would depart from them. Soon they would begin to comprehend the ministry of the Holy Spirit and the emergence of the church. As New Testament commentator F. F. Bruce states, "Instead of the political power which had formerly been the object of their ambitions, a power far greater and nobler would be theirs. When the Holy Spirit came upon them, Jesus assured them, they would be clothed with heavenly power. . . ."[3]

Jesus further told the disciples to remain in Jerusalem, and soon they would receive what the Father had promised. "'Which,' He said, 'you heard of from Me; for John baptized with water, but you will be baptized with the Holy Spirit not many days from now'" (1:4–5).

What is the purpose? When Acts 1:1 is considered in light of Luke 1:3, it is likely that Acts continues Luke's purpose of providing "a certain Theophilus an accurate and orderly account of the origins of

Christianity, about which Theophilus had some information already."[4] Even though Theophilus was obviously an historical person, he also represented the middle-class literate Roman who must have been interested in learning the story about Christ.

Acts has been called *the Acts of the Apostles* and *the Acts of the Holy Spirit*. The central person in Luke's Gospel is Jesus. Peter is prominently mentioned in the first part of Acts, and then the focus shifts to Paul. However, Acts is not primarily biographical but the story of the movement of the church from Jerusalem to the ends of the earth.

Luke's Gospel and Acts give an account of the life and ministry of Jesus and the birth and expansion of the church. Acts is an historical record of the first-generation church, but it also inspires believers of every age to find their role in the mission of the church.

Promise (1:6–8)

Jesus promised the apostles they would be empowered to be his witnesses to the ends of the earth.

Who are the witnesses? Jesus said, "You shall be My witnesses" (1:6). To whom was Jesus referring? The apostles and those who were witnesses of the resurrected Jesus were included in this statement as were all who later were gathered together in the upper room in Jerusalem (1:13–15). Yet as the Book of Acts unfolds, we are aware that all of Christ's followers were empowered by God's Spirit to be witnesses. Acts 8:1 states that because of "severe persecution . . . the church in Jerusalem" was scattered "throughout the countryside of Judea and Samaria"—"all except

WITNESSES

Bible commentator William J. Larkin, Jr., states, "Jesus says to be His witnesses. To be a witness (*martys*) is to speak from personal knowledge of facts and their significance. The apostles, as eyewitnesses of the saving events, were witnesses in a unique sense. But all those who will believe and appropriate the truth of their testimony also qualify as witnesses."[7] All believers are called to be empowered by the Holy Spirit as witnesses of the transformational grace of Christ.

the apostles." Then in verse 4 we are told that the ones "who were scattered went from place to place, proclaiming the word." The expansion of the church did not come through the proclamation of a few disciples (or preachers) but through the men and women empowered by the Holy Spirit who were scattered throughout the world.

Why are we witnesses? We are all to be Christ's witnesses *because Christ has commanded us to be.* In Matthew 28:19–20 the church is commanded to make disciples of all the nations. In Acts 1:8 we are commanded to be witnesses to the most remote part of the earth.

We are also witnesses because of the *urgent need of the world.* The Gospel of Luke states that Jesus' mission was "to seek and to save that which was lost" (Luke 19:10). Just before Jesus' ascension, Jesus told the apostles they were his witnesses "and that repentance for forgiveness of sins would be proclaimed in His name to all the nations, beginning from Jerusalem" (Luke 24:47–48). The work of the Savior became the work of the church.

People have rebelled against God and chosen a lifestyle of self-destruction since the fall of Adam. We are incapable of restoring ourselves. Each generation finds new ways to bring destruction to the earth, to our bodies, and to our relationships. The church must proclaim the hope of Christ because individually and collectively we desperately need him.

Further, we are Jesus' witnesses *because our nature has been changed through our trust in him.* How can we not tell others what Christ is doing in our lives? The apostles had seen Jesus dead, and they had seen him when he was raised. Why should they be afraid of earthly rulers when they followed One who has the power over life and death? Note that Jesus did not command them to witness. Rather Jesus said *they would be* witnesses. Being a witness for Jesus is what a disciple does. Further, being a witness of Christ was not merely talking about Jesus. Rather their whole lives became testimonies.

What is the message? Jesus said, "You shall be *My* witnesses" (Acts 1:8, italics for emphasis). The message for the church to proclaim is *Christ.* In Acts 8:5, we learn of Philip "proclaiming Christ." In Acts 8:12, "they believed Philip preaching the good news about the kingdom of God and the name of Jesus Christ. . . ." When Philip met the eunuch from Ethiopia "beginning from this Scripture he preached Jesus to him" (8:35).

The goal of the church is not church growth. Evangelism is not talking about churches' programs, staffs, facilities, or ministries. *Evangelism*

IDENTIFYING YOUR KINGDOM ASSIGNMENT

- Who are three people who are already in your circle of relationships who give no evidence of knowing Christ?
- What will be your strategy for being Christ's witness with them?
- Is there a people group within your community for whom there is no evangelical church?
- Who are your church's ministry partners who are taking the hope of Christ to the ends of the earth?
- What is your part in supporting them?

is proclaiming Christ in the power of the Holy Spirit. Witnessing of Christ was not an occasional activity in which the early church participated. They were witnesses of Christ with their lifestyles. Their speech, lifestyle, and conduct spoke of their allegiance to Christ.

What is the strategy? Jesus said they were to be his witnesses "in Jerusalem, and in all Judea and Samaria, and even to the remotest part of the earth" (1:8). We can view this strategy both geographically and relationally. As New Testament scholar F. F. Bruce comments, "It has often been pointed out that the geographical terms of v. 8 provide a sort of 'Index of Contents' for Acts. 'You shall be my witnesses' might be regarded as the theme of the book; 'in Jerusalem' covers the first seven chapters; 'in all Judea and Samaria' chapters 8:1—11:18; and the remainder of the book deals with the progress of the gospel outside the frontiers of the Holy Land until at last it reaches Rome."[5]

Geographically we are to begin right where we are in our location. If we fail to reach our own community, then who will? Yet we must also remember that billions of people have not even heard this message of salvation. The promise and assignment of Acts 1:8 is for the church of each generation to be witnesses "even to the remotest part of the earth" (1:8).

In his book *Concentric Circles of Concern,* Oscar Thompson illustrates that the gospel typically follows relationships. So the mission mandate can be understood relationally. Jerusalem is our home. Our strategy moves us from family to friends and even to enemies (Samaritans) and to the strangers we are yet to meet.

Implications and Actions

We must pay attention to Jesus' message in Acts 1:8. Being Jesus' witnesses is our job, too. We must not be lulled to sleep by universalism (the notion that everyone will be saved) or by thinking evangelism—witnessing—is just the role of a select few. It is "the church's number one job."[6] Is it yours?

QUESTIONS

1. What did Jesus mean when he said we would be his "witnesses"?

2. What is the role of the Holy Spirit in missions?

3. How does the promise in Acts 1:8 relate to you and your church?

4. Where is your Jerusalem, Judea, Samaria, and beyond?

NOTES ──────────────────────────────────────

1. Unless otherwise indicated, all Scripture quotations in lessons 1–2 are taken from the New American Standard Bible (1995 edition).

2. William J. Larkin, Jr., *Acts*, The IVP New Testament Commentary Series (Downers Grove, Illinois: InterVarsity Press, 1995), 17.

3. F. F. Bruce, *The Book of Acts*, The New International Commentary on the New Testament (Grand Rapids, Michigan: William B. Eerdmans Publishing Co., 1983), 38.

4. Bruce, 19.

5. Bruce, 39.

6. Larkin, 14.

7. Larkin, 41–42.

FOCAL TEXT
Acts 1:12–14; 2:1–18

BACKGROUND
Acts 1:12—2:36

MAIN IDEA
The Holy Spirit empowered Jesus' followers to witness to and minister for Jesus.

QUESTION TO EXPLORE
What actions are we undertaking that require the Spirit's power rather than simply our own human efforts?

STUDY AIM
To evaluate the extent to which I am truly relying on the Spirit's power in being Jesus' witness

QUICK READ
God has tasked his followers to be a global witness—a commission that is beyond our ability. Thankfully, God has also promised to fully empower us for the task.

LESSON TWO
Rely On the Power of God's Spirit

Imagine a day without power. Not *some* day back in history during the times of candles and horse-drawn carriages. Imagine one of *your* days without power. No electrical power. No battery power.

How would you start your day without the alarm clock plugged into your wall? What would your day look like with no cell phones, computers, or other electronics? What would you look like with no electric shavers, hair dryers, irons, or running water?

Assuming you could make it to work, without power, could you still do your job? No power drills. No copiers. You would no longer be able to respond to the hundreds of texts, calls, faxes, and e-mails you may get on a normal day. Would you write notes or letters instead?

Even lunch time would look unfamiliar in a powerless world. No electric ovens. No microwaves. No orders in the drive-through lane at the fast food place. You could not call in a pizza for delivery.

Continue to imagine your life without power. No smart phones. No GPS. No debit card purchases and no ATM transactions. No MP3 players or CD players. No streaming movies or cable television. Your books would have to be the paper kind—no electronic books for your tablet or book reader. Who would answer your questions when Google or other internet search engines aren't around?

At this point, you may be saying, *I can't imagine living a life without power!*

Equally unimaginable is attempting to live a spiritual life without power. You don't have to.[1]

ACTS 1:12–14

12 Then they returned to Jerusalem from the mount called Olivet, which is near Jerusalem, a Sabbath day's journey away. 13 When they had entered the city, they went up to the upper room where they were staying; that is, Peter and John and James and Andrew, Philip and Thomas, Bartholomew and Matthew, James the son of Alphaeus, and Simon the Zealot, and Judas the son of James. 14 These all with one mind were continually devoting themselves to prayer, along with the women, and Mary the mother of Jesus, and with His brothers.

ACTS 2:1–18

[1] When the day of Pentecost had come, they were all together in one place. [2] And suddenly there came from heaven a noise like a violent rushing wind, and it filled the whole house where they were sitting. [3] And there appeared to them tongues as of fire distributing themselves, and they rested on each one of them. [4] And they were all filled with the Holy Spirit and began to speak with other tongues, as the Spirit was giving them utterance. [5] Now there were Jews living in Jerusalem, devout men from every nation under heaven. [6] And when this sound occurred, the crowd came together, and were bewildered because each one of them was hearing them speak in his own language. [7] They were amazed and astonished, saying, "Why, are not all these who are speaking Galileans? [8] "And how is it that we each hear them in our own language to which we were born? [9] "Parthians and Medes and Elamites, and residents of Mesopotamia, Judea and Cappadocia, Pontus and Asia, [10] Phrygia and Pamphylia, Egypt and the districts of Libya around Cyrene, and visitors from Rome, both Jews and proselytes, [11] Cretans and Arabs—we hear them in our own tongues speaking of the mighty deeds of God." [12] And they all continued in amazement and great perplexity, saying to one another, "What does this mean?" [13] But others were mocking and saying, "They are full of sweet wine." [14] But Peter, taking his stand with the eleven, raised his voice and declared to them: "Men of Judea and all you who live in Jerusalem, let this be known to you and give heed to my words. [15] "For these men are not drunk, as you suppose, for it is only the third hour of the day; 16 but this is what was spoken of through the prophet Joel: [17] `And it shall be in the last days,' God says, `That I will pour forth of My Spirit on all mankind; And your sons and your daughters shall prophesy, And your young men shall see visions, And your old men shall dream dreams; [18] Even on My bondslaves, both men and women, I will in those days pour forth of My Spirit And they shall prophesy. . . .'"

The Power of Purposeful Waiting (1:12–14)

Before Jesus' ascension, he gathered his followers and gave them a simple command—"Wait" (Acts 1:4). *Simple,* however, does not mean *easy.* Waiting can be frustrating. We seldom find value in waiting. Waiting feels unproductive. Yet, waiting was part of God's plan for empowering his followers.

The key to waiting is to wait with purpose. The disciples did not accidentally wait. They obediently waited. The obedience was not only *that* they waited but *how* they waited.

Acts 1:14 tells us that the disciples all waited "with one mind." What an interesting description for a group of people who had experienced so much. They went through the traumatic transition of a ministry marked with revolutionary teaching and miraculous works. They watched the brutal public death of their leader. Suddenly, their hopes were revived with the resurrected Messiah. What was in their minds that united them in their waiting?

Jesus' command to "wait" had been accompanied by a purpose. "Wait for what the Father had promised" (1:4). Often the only thing that makes waiting bearable is knowing what comes after the waiting. After the wait came the promise—"you will be baptized with the Holy Spirit not many days from now" (1:5). The Father declared the promise. The Son reinforced the promise—"which you heard from me" (1:4).

The purpose for the waiting was the promise. "You will receive power when the Holy Spirit has come upon you; and you shall be My witnesses" (1:8). The purpose for the promise was the power. The promise would change the waiting disciples. The disciples would change the waiting world.

One command, followed by one promise, resulted in the disciples waiting with one mind.

Have you ever noticed something in common about the places we routinely have to wait? These places provide means to fill our time while we wait. The magazines in the doctor's waiting room, the game on the television at the barbershop, and the music in the elevators are all supposed to give us something to do while we wait.

What do you do when you find yourself in the waiting rooms of life? when you are between jobs? between ministries? between stages of life?

Are you trying to find things that will fill your time as you transition from one season in your life to another?

Sometimes we resign ourselves to a self-imposed pattern of how God works in our lives. God does something in me. I wait. God moves again in my life. I wait. I wait some more. God does something again. And I'm back to waiting for the next move of God.

Waiting is not a *pause* in the process of God's work in our lives.

Waiting is a *part* of the process of God's work in our lives.

How can we maximize the *wait time* in our lives? By following the disciples' example. The followers of Jesus purposefully filled their waiting time. They "were continually devoting themselves to prayer" (1:14).

What are you waiting for? Pray.

The Power of Promise and Provision (2:1–13)

The wait was over. The day of Pentecost had come (2:1).

To celebrate the day of Pentecost was to celebrate God's promise and provision. In that respect, this Pentecost would be no different for Jesus' Jewish disciples. They would celebrate promise. They would celebrate provision.

But this Pentecost would also be like no other. First came the noise like a rushing wind. Then the tongues of fire rested on each of those present. Finally, the Spirit filled the followers and gave them utterance (2:2–4).

Not surprisingly, the Jews living in Jerusalem were "amazed and astonished" (2:7). However, the noise that filled the house had not caused their amazement. Neither had the divine pyrotechnics. What did those first Christians do that caused the observers to continue "in amazement and great perplexity" (2:12)? We don't have to guess. The Bible is clear. They heard the Christian disciples "speaking of the mighty deeds of God" (2:11).

Christians speaking about the works of God—that sounds neither challenging nor impressive. That is, until you have to share your praise report in the native tongue of "Parthians and Medes and Elamites, and residents of Mesopotamia, Judea and Cappadocia, Pontus and Asia, Phrygia and Pamphylia, Egypt and the districts of Libya around Cyrene, and visitors from Rome, both Jews and proselytes, Cretans and Arabs" (2:9–11).

Such a testimonial witness is possible when you have a promise and provision. The disciples at Pentecost had both. Jesus had commanded them to "wait for what the Father had promised" (1:4) and they would "receive power when the Holy Spirit has come upon you; and you shall be My witnesses both in Jerusalem, and in all Judea and Samaria, and even to the remotest part of the earth" (1:8).

Without the divine power to witness, the believers would be quickly derailed in their efforts to witness to such a diverse crowd. In such a complex context, the gospel would be lost in translation. Take the Parthians, Medes, Elamites, the residents of Mesopotamia, and the Arabs. They were from areas located in modern Iran, Iraq, Saudi Arabia, and Yemen. Yet, the Holy Spirit gave the believers power to witness across geo-political boundaries. Also present were Asians (the Roman province of Asia), Egyptians, and visitors from Rome. The Holy Spirit's power would prove

PENTECOST, PROMISE, AND PROVISION

To arrive at Pentecost, the journey begins with the Passover celebration. Fifty days would be marked according to God's command (Leviticus 23:16). This period of seven full weeks concluded with the celebration of *Shavuot*—the Festival of Weeks. Because the celebration was on the fiftieth day, it became known as Pentecost.

Initially, the celebration was marked by grain offerings, burnt offerings, drink offerings, and peace offerings (Lev. 23:16–19). Work was prohibited. Later, the Jewish people included the customs of reading the Book of Ruth and eating a meal consisting of dairy products.

God had been clear about where and when the first *Shavuot* was to be celebrated—"When you enter the land which I am going to give to you and reap its harvest" (Lev. 23:10). Not *if*, but *when*. "*When* you enter" and "*when* . . . you reap" (italics added for emphasis). God was sure that the Land of Promise would yield its fruitful harvest.

To celebrate the day of Pentecost was to celebrate God's promise and provision.

effective in overcoming the linguistic barriers to "speaking the mighty deeds of God" (2:11).

The result of the promise and provision was power to witness.

The Power of the Spirit and You (2:14–18)

The Holy Spirit's display of power in the believers left some observers amazed and others confused. Some even mocked the believers and accused them of being drunk. Peter stepped in and explained what was going on.

Quoting Joel 2:28–32, Peter reminded the crowd about God's promise to pour forth his Spirit on all people. God's specificity is both encouraging and encompassing. "All mankind" (2:17). His empowering would include "sons" and "daughters," "young men" and "old men," "men and women" servants (Acts 2:17–18).

God's pouring out his Spirit at Pentecost was not only the fulfillment of a prophecy and a promise. It was also the natural progression in God's pattern of empowering those he sends out.

Before Jesus began his public ministry, he made a declaration in the synagogue. "The Spirit of the Lord is upon Me, Because He anointed Me to preach the gospel to the poor. He has sent Me to proclaim release to the captives, And recovery of sight to the blind, To set free those who are oppressed, To proclaim the favorable year of the Lord" (Luke 4:18).

In short, Jesus was empowered to preach the gospel and to minister.

When Jesus sent out the Twelve, he "gave them power and authority over all the demons and to heal diseases. And He sent them out to proclaim the kingdom of God and to perform healing" (Luke 9:1–2). The Twelve were empowered to preach the gospel and to minister.

Jesus then sent out a group of seventy. He instructed them to heal those "who are sick, and say to them, 'The kingdom of God has come near to you'" (Luke 10:9). They were able to complete their mission because Jesus had given them authority (Luke 10:19). The seventy were empowered to preach the gospel and to minister.

At Pentecost, the Spirit empowered one hundred twenty believers. Later that day, Peter said to them, "Repent, and each of you be baptized in the name of Jesus Christ for the forgiveness of your sins; and you will

---

CASE STUDY

For many years, Jim was very active in one of your church's minis-tries. Several months ago, he resigned, saying that God had *called him away* from that ministry. Since then, he hasn't gotten involved in ministry in any meaningful way. When you ask him about serving, he says, *I'm waiting on God to lead me.* Besides prayer, what would you recommend that Jim do so that he can make the most of his waiting time?

---

receive the gift of the Holy Spirit" (Acts 2:38). As a result, 3,000 people received Jesus' word and were baptized.

Jesus was empowered. Then the Twelve were empowered. Then the seventy. Followed by one hundred twenty and then three thousand. How about you?

Peter reminds us that the promise of the Holy Spirit "is for you and your children and for all who are far off, as many as the Lord our God will call to Himself" (2:39). Have you repented? Have you received the Holy Spirit? Has the Lord called you to himself?

You too can be empowered to witness and to minister. The promise is for you.

Implications and Actions

At times, God calls us to the unassuming adventure of waiting on him. The wait is part of God's process in our divine formation and is especially effective when we devote our waiting time to prayer. The celebration of Pentecost was marked by both promise and provision. Jesus had instructed his followers to wait for both. The Father's promise of the Holy Spirit's power was fulfilled. The Spirit was the necessary provision of power for the early followers of Christ. The promise and the reality of the Spirit's power are also for us. We too can be empowered to be Jesus' witnesses and ministers.

QUESTIONS

1. Remember our exercise in which we imagined a day without power? A powerless existence does not compare to a life lived with power. Why do you think some people try to live their spiritual lives without power?

2. Think of a time when you believed you were *waiting on God*. How did you feel? What did you do while you waited?

3. If the disciples had not occupied themselves with continual prayer, what do you imagine they would have done instead?

4. Have you experienced a time when you have celebrated God's promise or provision in your life?

5. Is there something you have not done that would be possible with the Spirit's power at work in you?

NOTES ————————————————————————————

1. Unless otherwise indicated, all Scripture quotations in lessons 1–2 are taken from the New American Standard Bible (1995 edition).

FOCAL TEXT
Acts 3:1–10

BACKGROUND
Acts 3

MAIN IDEA
Jesus' followers witnessed
by caring for all the needs
of people—physical as
well as spiritual.

QUESTION TO EXPLORE
What needs of people
does God care about?

STUDY AIM
To decide on ways I will
respond to all the needs
of people—physical as
well as spiritual

QUICK READ
Christ's followers should look
for opportunities to imitate
Jesus' holistic compassion for
humanity by meeting people's
physical needs and verbally
communicating the gospel
for their spiritual needs.

LESSON THREE

Engage in Holistic Witness for Jesus

Having received the Holy Spirit (Acts 2), Peter and John were ready to act in the Spirit's power by serving as Christ's witnesses beginning in Jerusalem (Luke 24:49, 53; Acts 1:8). But not only as verbal witnesses of the gospel. They'd seen their compassionate Lord Jesus heal physical maladies while traveling through towns and villages (Matthew 15:30–31; Mark 2:5, 11; Luke 7:22; John 5:3–9). His twelve disciples, including Peter and John, walked with him, and saw and experienced his interaction with those to whom he proclaimed the "good news of the kingdom" and healed of "every disease and sickness" (Matt. 9:35).[1] They observed firsthand Christ's love for humanity's spiritual and physical well-being (Matt. 9:36). Furthermore, they presumably experienced the joy of helping people when Jesus gave the Twelve "authority to drive out impure spirits and to heal every disease and sickness" (Matt. 10:1).

This holistic approach to ministry is our model today. Jesus values the *complete* person, and we should, too. His love for humanity spans our entire being. He doesn't compartmentalize our lives into the spiritual, the physical, the mental, and the emotional. Neither should we. We are each more than the mere sum of our parts. We are living beings created in the image of the Almighty God, and every aspect of our creation has worth and value. Thus, the physical infirmities we battle are also of supreme importance to him.

The need Peter and John encountered at the temple was not an extraordinary or unusual one for their day and time. Likewise, we daily encounter needs that offer opportunities to engage in witness and ministry holistically. The question is: Do we recognize those opportunities when they arise?

ACTS 3:1–10

[1] One day Peter and John were going up to the temple at the time of prayer—at three in the afternoon. [2] Now a man who was lame from birth was being carried to the temple gate called Beautiful, where he was put every day to beg from those going into the temple courts. [3] When he saw Peter and John about to enter, he asked them for money. [4] Peter looked straight at him, as did John. Then Peter said, "Look at us!" [5] So the man gave them his attention, expecting to get something from them.

> [6] Then Peter said, "Silver or gold I do not have, but what I do have I give you. In the name of Jesus Christ of Nazareth, walk." [7] Taking him by the right hand, he helped him up, and instantly the man's feet and ankles became strong. [8] He jumped to his feet and began to walk. Then he went with them into the temple courts, walking and jumping, and praising God. [9] When all the people saw him walking and praising God, [10] they recognized him as the same man who used to sit begging at the temple gate called Beautiful, and they were filled with wonder and amazement at what had happened to him.

Not Just Another Day at the Temple (3:1–5)

Just because the early Christians in Jerusalem were followers of Jesus Christ—"the Way" (Acts 9:2; 24:14)—didn't mean they'd abandoned the roots of their Jewish heritage. Peter and John, along with other believers, "continued to meet together in the temple courts" (2:46), and as recorded by Luke, were on this day "going up to the temple to pray" (3:1) at one of the traditional hours (see small article, "Time to Pray"). Out of reverence and respect, going to the temple was always spoken of as "going up" (see Luke 18:10; John 7:14). It was also a literal description, for there were numerous ascending terraces within the complex, and the temple itself was on a hill (2 Chronicles 3:1). Therefore, visitors went "up" from any direction!

As Peter and John walked, they encountered a man "over forty years old" (Acts 4:22) who was "crippled from birth" (3:2). Luke mentioned near the end of the previous chapter that "many wonders and signs were done by the apostles" (2:43). As evidence, he told how these two men served as God's instruments in the performance of a miracle of healing for this disabled man, and thereby set the stage for the opposition and persecution the church would experience.

The man's healing was particularly remarkable when considered in light of his age and having never been able to walk. Furthermore, he was so significantly crippled he could not even hobble to his destination at the temple. He had to be carried every day (3:2). According to levitical law and tradition, he had little significance in Jewish society.

Peter and John were attending the temple at the time of the grain/flour-offering, a gift offering of food, and yet this man was not allowed to present such an offering because of his malady (see Leviticus 21:17–20). Up to this point, his life's goal was merely survival, and he could best accomplish that by begging for alms (money given as a gift to the poor). Because giving alms was viewed as a virtuous act, strategically placing himself at the temple gate was a great place for repentant sinners to give, hoping God would take notice and ascribe merit to them for their act of benevolent generosity.

There is some debate about the location of the "Beautiful" Gate where the crippled man sat. It was likely either the gate leading from the court

TIME TO PRAY

Three prayer services with specific names and functions were recited daily with two accompanied by sacrifices in the temple courts, as follows:

- *Shaharit* (from Hebrew *shahar* meaning *morning light*) was the first hour of prayer when the temple gates opened at 9 a.m. During this time, burnt offerings of various meats were given, and worshipers expressed trust in God for the day ahead.

- *Minhah* was the afternoon hour of prayer, approximately 3 p.m. Requiring no bloodshed, typically an offering of cakes was presented. The offering was made of flour, oil, salt and spices, but without yeast. It was also known as the *hour of confession*.

- *Ma'arib*, derived from the Hebrew word for *nightfall*, generally occurred at or just after sundown, when three stars were visible. This prayer was intended for committing oneself to God's service for the next day.

Prayers such as the *Shema* (see Deuteronomy 6:4–9) or *Kaddish* (a doxology) were generally spoken in unison among those present, but most other prayers were led by one person while the congregation responded with "Amen."[7]

of the Gentiles (where all people were welcome) into the court of women (where only Jews were permitted), or the gate leading from the court of women into the court of Israel (where only Jewish men were allowed). Depending on the resource referenced, both of these gates have been given the label of Nicanor Gate. The name is only significant because the first-century Jewish historian Josephus claimed the Nicanor Gate was of exquisite workmanship beautifully overlaid with Corinthian bronze.[2] It seems likely the lame man would choose a location to beg from the largest audience, which would indicate the gate leading from the court of the Gentiles to the court of women.[3]

In response to the beggar's request for money, Peter clearly recognized an opportunity for ministry and the proclamation of the gospel. So, looking steadfastly (Greek *atenisas*, like our English *attentively*) at the crippled man, he said, "Look at us!" (Acts 3:4). Thinking he had a benefactor, the beggar looked up expectantly (3:5). He probably believed he was about to receive a substantial financial gift for Peter to desire his undivided attention.

Better Than He Expected (3:6–10)

As Peter and the man made eye contact, the idiomatic expression for currency, "silver and gold," surely captured his attention (3:6). However, what came next certainly wasn't what he was expecting. In fact, he probably had a rather disheartened expression when Peter told him he had no money to give! One wonders what the man thought as Peter then instructed, "In the name of Jesus Christ of Nazareth, walk" (3:6). Likely the man had seen Jesus in and around the temple teaching (Luke 19:47) and healing (Matt. 21:14). Perhaps he'd even witnessed Jesus clear the courts of those who exchanged currency and sold doves (see Mark 11:15; Luke 19:45). However, we have no indication the lame man even believed Jesus was a good teacher, much less the Messiah in whom he should place his faith.

Peter's use of the authority of the name of Jesus was deliberate in its purpose and meaning. First, Peter demonstrated the compassion modeled by Christ by simply meeting a physical need before preaching the gospel.

Second, by instructing the man, "In the name of Jesus Christ of Nazareth, walk," Peter indicated the one performing the healing. Jewish culture used names not merely to identify a person but also to express the person's very nature, meaning the power of the person was present and available by using the name of the person. "Peter, therefore, [asked] the risen Jesus to heal [and pronounced] over the crippled beggar [Jesus'] name and power (cf. 4:10)."[4] Peter expounded on this in his sermon, explaining, "It is Jesus' name and the faith that comes through him that has given this complete healing to him" (3:16). Calling on Jesus' name was quite common in Acts, as the apostles dealt with diseases, demon possessions, deformities, and sin, and in so doing almost always brought evangelistic opportunities resulting in people's salvation.

Finally, Peter was very specific in his identification of this One whose authority he claimed: "Jesus Christ of Nazareth." He wanted there to be no doubt of Jesus' divinity by mentioning "Christ" (Hebrew and Aramaic *Messiah,* meaning *anointed one*). Too, he wanted no confusion about which Jesus he meant (the one from Nazareth who taught, preached, and was executed prior to this event). The resultant miracle served as further evidence Jesus was now resurrected and his impact would not be suppressed.

Having commanded the man to "walk" (3:6), Peter offered the lame man his hand to help raise him to his feet (3:7). The man's feet and ankles were strengthened immediately. Instantaneous healing occurred, not a gradual improvement over a period of time.

HERE AND THERE

Many believers are more comfortable ministering and sharing their faith *away* from familiar faces and places. While Jesus certainly commanded us to be his witnesses "to the ends of the earth" (Acts 1:8), he instructed us to begin where we are. Peter and John model being Christ's witnesses even in areas with which they were most familiar. Consider:

- How willing are you to get involved in ministry and evangelism at home?
- What do you believe are your strengths, talents, and/or giftings?
- With whom or what ministry can you partner?
- Will you ask someone to keep you accountable in this area?

As the beggar recognized his newfound strength, he not only stood, but he "jumped to his feet" and began walking (3:8)! Striding alongside Peter and John, he demonstrated the healing power of God in his life by also jumping, fulfilling the Messianic prophecy of Isaiah 35:6: "Then will the lame leap like a deer." Next, this man who had never been permitted to offer a grain-offering sacrifice entered the temple courts and offered a sacrifice of praise by verbally praising God, recognizing his healing as a divine act. His words of celebration may have been mere announcements of divine adoration, but it is possible he was expressing himself musically as well, since Luke used the same word for praise in this verse and in Acts 2:47 (*aineo*) where the implication is corporate worship in song.

The surrounding crowd, which would have been of significant size, since this was a common hour of prayer and sacrifice, immediately began to take notice of the excitement (Acts 3:9), and recognized him as the formerly lame man who'd begged at the gate (3:10). They knew he'd been genuinely crippled, not a fraud seeking financial gain, and they were astonished (Greek *thambos,* meaning *reverentially fearful*) and amazed (Greek, *ekstasis*). However, awe does not constitute salvation or faith. Peter and John capitalized on the interest aroused at the man's healing by seizing the opportunity to share the good news of Christ's gospel immediately as they stood in Solomon's Colonnade (3:11).

Verses 11 and following describe Peter's message. He specified Jesus' fulfillment of prophecy, identified him as the Messiah (3:13–18), and called the people to repentance (3:19–20, 26). In fact, in 4:9, the word used by Peter to describe the change in the man's condition, frequently translated "healed," is the word *sozo,* meaning *saved.* Thus, the man was *saved* from his crippled condition, and then he and those around him were offered the opportunity to be *saved* from sin. The healing act without the message of the gospel would have accomplished only part of God's purpose and plan.

Eyes to See

To be a holistic witness for Christ in modern culture, we are to see people saved not only from their physical and emotional circumstances of need, but we must also offer them the eternal, life-giving message of salvation from sin and separation from God.

Many churches and denominations have means of meeting human needs. From soup kitchens to hospitals to orphanages, your local church body probably financially supports ministries similar to these, and may even encourage volunteer participation.

Yet, as it was for Peter and John, people you encounter in your daily life have physical or emotional needs you can meet, thus opening lines of communication for sharing a verbal witness about the hope you've found in Christ. The *barista* (server) at the coffee shop may be a college student who could use a better tip. Your single-parent neighbor might appreciate you keeping the kids while he or she goes to the store. What if you sat with that co-worker in the break room who always sits alone? or sent an e-mail of encouragement to a prodigal member of your family? A listening ear coupled with a Scripture verse might be just what the delivery person craves. Each of these acts agrees with what Mother Teresa said: "Find the sick, the suffering and the lonely right there where you are . . . if you have the eyes to see."[5]

QUESTIONS

1. Peter and John faced opposition and persecution after they fulfilled God's purpose in this man's life (Acts 4:1–3, 18, 21). Obedience to the call of Christ means risking misunderstanding, mistreatment, and even oppression. How will you prepare yourself for these risks?

2. Whom does the Lord bring to mind as you consider someone you know who needs a personal touch of hope and healing? Will you be that touch of salvation in his or her life? What will you do?

3. What physical and/or emotional ministries does your church fellowship offer or support? Can you think of other ministries needed in your community in order to help people and reach them with the gospel? Do you sense God's calling to be a catalyst for beginning something new?

4. On the scale below, in one color of ink mark where you believe your church fellowship falls in meeting physical needs and verbally sharing the gospel message. Then, in another color ink, mark where you are personally.

| Meeting only physical needs | Only verbally sharing the Gospel message |

5. If Peter had not extended his hand to help the lame man get up, do you think he would have tried to stand on his own? Why or why not? Would you have been willing to risk the faith it took to stand?

6. In a first-century world filled with fears of diseases, demons, and magic, the impact of the kind of evangelism Peter and John did in Acts 3 was very significant. Such phenomena done in Jesus' name proved to be superior to the cures and exorcisms of pagan physicians and magicians.[6] Many claim these miracles don't occur in the twenty-first century. How have you seen God's healing power demonstrated, and what was the evangelistic impact of those circumstances?

NOTES

1. Unless otherwise indicated, all Scripture quotations in lessons 3–4, 6–8, 10–13 are taken from The Holy Bible, New International Version (North American Edition), copyright © 1973, 1978, 1984 by the International Bible Society.

2. F.F. Bruce, *The Book of Acts,* New International Commentary on the New Testament (Grand Rapids, MI: William B. Eerdmans Publishing Company, 1988), 77.

3. For this reason some scholars suggest the "Beautiful" Gate was perhaps even the exterior *Shushan* (or Golden) Gate at the eastern wall of the temple complex and old Jerusalem.

4. Richard N. Longnecker, "The Acts of the Apostles," *Expositor's Bible Commentary,* vol. 9, ed. Frank E. Gaebelein (Grand Rapids, MI: Zondervan, 1981), 294.

5. Mary Poplin, *Finding Calcutta* (Downers Grove, IL: InterVarsity Press, 2008), back cover.

6. D.S. Lim, "Evangelism in the Early Church," *Dictionary of the Later New Testament,* ed. Ralph P. Martin and Peter H. Davids (Downers Grove, IL: InterVarsity Press, 1997), 356.

7. Compiled from the articles "Prayer," "Ma'arib," "Sacrifice," "Shema," "Minhah," and "Kaddish," accessed 1/10/2012 at http://www.jewishencyclopedia.com, and from the articles "Maariv," "Minchah," and "Shacharit–Morning Prayers," accessed 1/12/2012 at http://www.chabad.org.

FOCAL TEXT
Acts 4:5–31

BACKGROUND
Acts 4

MAIN IDEA
The disciples prayed for and exercised boldness in serving as Jesus' witnesses.

QUESTION TO EXPLORE
How can we exercise greater boldness in serving as Jesus' witnesses?

STUDY AIM
To decide on ways I will exercise greater boldness in serving as Jesus' witness

QUICK READ
Peter and John boldly resisted the pressure of the religious leaders to stop them from obeying God, and they continued to proclaim the word of God about Jesus.

LESSON FOUR
Pray for Boldness in Being Jesus' Witness

During my formative years, I would experience bouts of silence, especially when I was being introduced to adults. Often my mother, grandmother, or someone else would say: *I guess the cat's got his tongue.* This expression, common decades ago, was directed at anyone who was quiet when expected to speak. In that era, the statement was something one would say to a bashful or silent person in an attempt to get him or her to speak.

In Acts 4, Peter and John displayed the complete opposite of shyness and silence. Their ability and willingness to speak was a pivotal point in the spread of the good news in the early days of the church.[1]

ACTS 4:5–31

[5] The next day the rulers, the elders and the teachers of the law met in Jerusalem. [6] Annas the high priest was there, and so were Caiaphas, John, Alexander and others of the high priest's family. [7] They had Peter and John brought before them and began to question them: "By what power or what name did you do this?"

[8] Then Peter, filled with the Holy Spirit, said to them: "Rulers and elders of the people! [9] If we are being called to account today for an act of kindness shown to a man who was lame and are being asked how he was healed, [10] then know this, you and all the people of Israel: It is by the name of Jesus Christ of Nazareth, whom you crucified but whom God raised from the dead, that this man stands before you healed. [11] Jesus is

"'the stone you builders rejected,
which has become the cornerstone.'

[12] Salvation is found in no one else, for there is no other name under heaven given to mankind by which we must be saved."

[13] When they saw the courage of Peter and John and realized that they were unschooled, ordinary men, they were astonished and they took note that these men had been with Jesus. [14] But since they could see the man who had been healed standing there with them, there was nothing they could say. [15] So they ordered them to withdraw from the Sanhedrin and then conferred together. [16] "What are we going to do with these men?" they asked. "Everyone living in Jerusalem knows they have performed a notable sign, and we cannot deny it. [17] But to stop this thing from

spreading any further among the people, we must warn them to speak no longer to anyone in this name."

[18] Then they called them in again and commanded them not to speak or teach at all in the name of Jesus. [19] But Peter and John replied, "Which is right in God's eyes: to listen to you, or to him? You be the judges! [20] As for us, we cannot help speaking about what we have seen and heard."

[21] After further threats they let them go. They could not decide how to punish them, because all the people were praising God for what had happened. [22] For the man who was miraculously healed was over forty years old.

[23] On their release, Peter and John went back to their own people and reported all that the chief priests and the elders had said to them. [24] When they heard this, they raised their voices together in prayer to God. "Sovereign Lord," they said, "you made the heavens and the earth and the sea, and everything in them. [25] You spoke by the Holy Spirit through the mouth of your servant, our father David:

"'Why do the nations rage
     and the peoples plot in vain?
[26] The kings of the earth rise up
     and the rulers band together
     against the Lord
     and against his anointed one.'

[27] Indeed Herod and Pontius Pilate met together with the Gentiles and the people of Israel in this city to conspire against your holy servant Jesus, whom you anointed. [28] They did what your power and will had decided beforehand should happen. [29] Now, Lord, consider their threats and enable your servants to speak your word with great boldness. [30] Stretch out your hand to heal and perform signs and wonders through the name of your holy servant Jesus."

[31] After they prayed, the place where they were meeting was shaken. And they were all filled with the Holy Spirit and spoke the word of God boldly.

Speaking Before the High Court (4:5–12)

This passage in Acts records the first persecution of the disciples of Jesus Christ. It came after the miraculous healing of the man crippled from birth at the temple gate (Acts 3; lesson 3). Peter and John were arrested while preaching. In spite of their arrest, the disciples grew in number to about 5,000. The next day these preachers found themselves standing before the Sanhedrin Council (Acts 4:5), the Jewish high court.

Peter and John were interrogated as criminals before this ruling body. The question focused on "what power" and "what name" (4:7). Peter and John had no legal or religious representation. They had no time to prepare a defense or call witnesses. One would expect them to be shaken in their spirits and intimidated. Even so, they were prepared for this moment. In John 15:18–27, before the Lord went to the cross, he informed them of the hatred and persecution to come. He also promised the Holy Spirit or "Counselor" who would enable them to witness about him (John 15:26–27).

Peter responded to the questions of the religious leaders. Being "filled with the Holy Spirit" (Acts 4:8), Peter spoke without hesitation or reservation and boldly proclaimed Jesus Christ as the source of healing power. As Peter gave his defense, he boldly reversed roles with the Sanhedrin. He charged the Sanhedrin with their role in Jesus' death, referring to "Jesus Christ of Nazareth, whom you crucified" (4:10). He immediately declared that God, in contrast, raised Jesus from the dead. Peter then boldly declared, "there is no other name under heaven given to mankind by which we must be saved" (4:12). *No* cat had *his* tongue!

THE SANHEDRIN

The Sanhedrin Council, the Jewish high court, was composed of seventy-one members including the high priest, who was the presiding officer. This high court was made up of three kinds of members: the chief priests; the elders; and the teachers of the law or scribes. The chief priests were wealthy and were the most powerful members of the Sanhedrin. They usually were Sadducees. The elders were distinguished laymen from the financial aristocracy. The teachers of the law or scribes were mostly Pharisees and were experts in the Jewish law.

Ordinary Men with Boldness (4:13–21)

Imagine the shock on the faces of the members of this imposing body of authoritative figures when they heard what Peter dared to say. The courage of Peter and John stunned them. They had witnessed Peter speaking publicly in front of them with "courage"—boldness, confidence, unshakable assurance (4:13).

The Sanhedrin Council noticed that these men had no formal training in the law. They had not attended any of the rabbinical schools. They had no certificates, no diplomas, no special commendations from religious authorities. They had been plain fishermen. These ordinary men however, were recognized by their interrogators with a distinguishing trait: "these men had been with Jesus" (4:13). Being with Jesus or knowing Jesus remains the qualifier for bold witnessing today.

Adding to this astonishment was that the man who had been healed was standing beside Peter and John, displaying the evidence of Jesus' power. This was a problem for the council. They conferred with one another outside the presence of Peter, John, and the living evidence. They were concerned with the numbers of people who were witnesses to the healing. The proof of healing was indisputable. So, motivated by fear and a desire to maintain their influence, they called and commanded Peter and John to "speak no longer to anyone in this name" (4:17).

Both Peter and John boldly responded, "we cannot help speaking about what we have seen and heard" (4:20). As Baptists, we honor the principles of soul competency and the priesthood of all believers. We believe and cherish religious liberty and oppose any right of government or a religious authority to impose on us silence or to coerce a confession of belief.

Peter and John spoke freely without fear. After being threatened, they were released even as people continuously praised God for the healing of the man "over forty years old" (4:22). The significance of identifying this man's age is found in the fact that the man had been crippled from birth. He had been seen for years begging at the temple gate. Now he was healed!

What an encouragement for us today! We can—and should—speak freely and boldly as witnesses for our Lord and Savior. Through the power of the Holy Spirit, we should have the same unshakable assurance to witness in all circumstances.

Believers Pray for Continued Boldness (4:23–31)

Peter and John returned to their community of believers. One should never underestimate the value of having a church, a believing community, in which to take refuge. Peter and John reported that they had been threatened not to preach or teach again in the name of Jesus. The company of believers responded with prayer. The threat came from the highest court, and so they called on Someone higher than the highest court. They appealed to a higher jurisdiction—God. They did not fear or complain; rather, they prayed.

It is important to note that their prayer meeting was not concentrated on buildings, beauty, bonuses, benefits, or blessings. They desired and prayed for *boldness* to keep spreading the good news of Jesus Christ. "Enable your servants to speak your word with great boldness. Stretch out your hand to heal and perform miraculous signs and wonders through the name of your holy servant Jesus" (4:29–30). Our communities and cities would change for the better if we prayed for boldness to witness.

What and how they prayed is instructive to us today when our witnessing is being threatened. Consider what and how they prayed.

1. They lifted their voices together (4:24). They prayed as one. There was unity of heart and spirit.

2. They prayed aloud! (4:24). They raised their voices because the stakes were high. This was no time to be timid during prayer.

3. They acknowledged God's sovereignty (4:24). God is Creator and Ruler.

4. They prayed Scripture during their crisis (4:25–26). They prayed Psalm 2:1–2, applying Scripture to their circumstances.

5. They requested continued boldness for proclaiming God's "word" in the face of threats (4:29). They were determined to spread the good news in disobedience to the Sanhedrin. They prayed for their leaders to maintain the boldness already demonstrated.

6. They desired the manifestation of God to continue in healings, signs, and wonders (4:30).

Implications and Actions

What boldness Peter and John displayed when challenged by the religious authorities! They had every reason to back down before the formidable Sanhedrin. There were only two of them facing seventy-one of the most powerful people in the land. But they "had been with Jesus," learning from him before the resurrection and experiencing his majesty afterward. At seventy-one to two, the Sanhedrin didn't know how vastly outnumbered they were.

There's no hint of arrogance or being obnoxious on the part of Peter and John. There's only the quiet conviction that "we cannot help speaking about what we have seen and heard" (4:20).

What a prayer meeting afterward! The boldness in prayer of Peter and John and their fellow church members prompted an affirmation from God assuring them that their prayer was heard and answered. The place was "shaken" (4:31). The place where they prayed *moved*. God's presence and power was evident and experienced by those in the prayer meeting. The result of the prayer meeting: " . . . They were all filled with the Holy Spirit and spoke the word of God boldly" (4:31).

The cat did not get their tongues! If we pray for boldness, God will grant it.

QUESTIONS

1. What enabled Peter and John to be bold for Jesus' sake?

2. How can we avoid being merely arrogant or obnoxious and calling it being bold for Jesus' sake?

3. How does *being practical* relate to being bold for Jesus' sake?

4. In what areas and opportunities is God encouraging you to be bold for Jesus' sake?

5. How does your church need to be more bold for Jesus' sake? What can you do to help and encourage?

NOTES

1. Unless otherwise indicated, all Scripture quotations in lessons 3–4, 6–8, 10–13 are taken from The Holy Bible, New International Version (North American Edition), copyright © 1973, 1978, 1984 by the International Bible Society.

FOCAL TEXT
Acts 6:1–7; 11:27–30

BACKGROUND
Acts 6:1–15; 8:1; 11:27–30; 12:25

MAIN IDEA
The early church extended help
to people in need, near and far.

QUESTION TO EXPLORE
How does ministry to
human need relate to
being Jesus' witnesses?

STUDY AIM
To plan to engage in at least
one action that will extend
my Christian witness by
ministering to human need

QUICK READ
All believers within the body
are called to be servants.
We must be willing to care
for those in need as well as
proclaim the gospel of Christ.

LESSON FIVE
Minister to Human Need

I remember my father's confession as we drove home from church thirty-five years ago. Between Sunday School and worship, men of the church would gather in the parking lot to discuss the week's events. Almost every man in my small country church was a coal miner. The men worked for different coal companies, and mines would shut down for various reasons.

My father had been out of work for some time. A friend at church quietly took him aside and asked whether he had enough money to feed his family. That gentle act of compassion moved my father to tears as he recounted the conversation during the car ride. There were other instances of generosity that sustained my family during difficult days. When I read today's focal text, I am reminded of the church of my childhood. Members of that tiny congregation took seriously God's command to care for those in need.[1]

ACTS 6:1-7

[1] Now during those days, when the disciples were increasing in number, the Hellenists complained against the Hebrews because their widows were being neglected in the daily distribution of food. [2] And the twelve called together the whole community of the disciples and said, "It is not right that we should neglect the word of God in order to wait on tables. [3] Therefore, friends, select from among yourselves seven men of good standing, full of the Spirit and of wisdom, whom we may appoint to this task, [4] while we, for our part, will devote ourselves to prayer and to serving the word." [5] What they said pleased the whole community, and they chose Stephen, a man full of faith and the Holy Spirit, together with Philip, Prochorus, Nicanor, Timon, Parmenas, and Nicolaus, a proselyte of Antioch. [6] They had these men stand before the apostles, who prayed and laid their hands on them.

[7] The word of God continued to spread; the number of the disciples increased greatly in Jerusalem, and a great many of the priests became obedient to the faith.

ACTS 11:27–30

[27] At that time prophets came down from Jerusalem to Antioch. [28] One of them named Agabus stood up and predicted by the Spirit that there would be a severe famine over all the world; and this took place during the reign of Claudius. [29] The disciples determined that according to their ability, each would send relief to the believers living in Judea; [30] this they did, sending it to the elders by Barnabas and Saul.

Address the Crisis and Make a Plan (6:1–4)

Acts 6 takes note of a developing problem in the church. The church was experiencing growing pains as it expanded rapidly. The Hellenist Jews (or Grecian Jews) felt their widows were not being cared for as well as the Hebraic Jewish widows. Grecian Jews were Jews who had lived in the Greek world but who had returned to Palestine. Likely they spoke Greek as opposed to Aramaic. New Testament scholar John Polhill says, "Diaspora Jews often moved to Jerusalem in their twilight years to die in the holy city."[2] Hellenist Jews would have been interacting with the secular world. Their outlook was vastly different from that of Hebraic Jews.

Caring for widows has been a hallmark of the Jewish faith. Visit Old Testament Scripture highlighting God's concern for this group (see Exodus 22:22–24; Deuteronomy 10:17–18; 14:28–29; Psalm 146:9). When the Grecian husbands died, there would be no one to care for their widows. Unlike the Hebraic Jews, their families were scattered. There may have been a large number of Hellenist widows in the church. Note that the Bible does not say the Hellenist widows were being deliberately discriminated against. Rather, with the rapid expansion of the church, they may have become an overlooked segment of the population. Ethnic tensions mounted, and there was a confrontation.

The apostles took care of the problem immediately. Although the complaint was issued by one group, they gathered the entire church to find a solution. The apostles chose a course of action that promoted unity.

On Acts 6:2, we cannot assume the text is implying that proclaiming "the word of God" is a more important or lofty task than caring for "the

DIASPORA, OR DISPERSION

Near the close of the Old Testament era, the Jews were ruled by Persia. Then Alexander defeated the Persians in 334 B.C. Alexander's quest was one civilization ruled by Greek culture.[11]

The Greek word *Diaspora* translates as *Dispersion*. The term is used for Jews living beyond Palestine.

Through the years, Jews were living abroad for a variety of reasons. New Testament scholar Ralph Martin says, "Outside of Palestine the Jews of the Dispersion were more pervasively exposed to Greek influences, which had the effect of liberalizing their religion and encouraging them to speak Greek."[12]

Often Greek principles and influences ran counter to Hebraic teachings and traditions. For example, Greeks promoted an uninhibited view of the naked human body. They esteemed physical prowess and prestige. Entertainment in the arena and theater became an integral part of life. The biggest affront to Hebraic Jews was Hellenist Jews forsaking the sacred Hebrew language for the Greek language.[13]

daily distribution of food" (6:1). This is rather about division of labor. All gifts are important in the body of Christ. Think about it for a moment. Why was it important for the apostles to minister the word? They were the ones who were actual witnesses to the life, death, and resurrection of Jesus Christ.[3] Interestingly, later in Acts we find that some of the seven selected for the task of helping the widows were preachers and evangelists, even being martyred for their faith.

The apostles asked the congregation to select men with honorable reputations who were filled with the Spirit and wise. This is a good place to start when identifying qualifications for current church roles. We must avoid the temptation to simply put names of willing appointees in open slots and call our work done.

Selecting the Seven (6:5–7)

Look carefully at the names of the seven men chosen for the ministry. All the names are Greek. There is other evidence to support that these men were Grecian or Hellenist Jews. They were likely leaders of the Hellenist group within the congregation.[4] They certainly would know how to best care for the Hellenist widows. Stephen's name is first. Later Acts describes Stephen's witness before the Sanhedrin and his death (Acts 6:8—7:60). Philip, the second on the list, became an important figure in the Acts narrative (8:4–40). We know Nicolas was not a Jew by birth. He was a convert from paganism to Judaism.[5]

Many interpret this passage to portray the selection of the first deacons. However, the Greek word for *deacon,* which is *diakonos,* never appears in the focal text. What does appear is the word for "ministry," or *diakonia.*[6] Therefore we should emphasize what they did rather than placing importance on a position of leadership.

The congregation presented their appointees to the apostles. The leaders were commissioned for a specific function through laying hands on them and through prayer. In the Old Testament, we see laying on of hands as a powerful symbol for bestowing a blessing. Jacob blessed the sons of Joseph by laying hands on them (Genesis 48:13–20), and Joshua was given a blessing in this way to become a leader (Numbers 27:23). In the New Testament, we find several instances where Jesus touched

LOVE ONE ANOTHER

Betty was working in one of the disaster relief feeding units in response to the recent Texas wildfires. Another volunteer was working the line with her. Officials came to find him. Firefighters had done all they could, but the wildfires had taken his home. Friends took up an offering of $200. Instead of spending the money on himself, the gentleman took the money and bought gift cards to give away at the shelter.

More money was donated. This time, he decided to go ahead and buy something for himself. He said to Betty, "With the money, I bought two tents; one for me to live in and one for a family at the shelter."

That is a beautiful picture of what it means to be a Christian. We are to love God and love others as much or more than we love ourselves. Often we are so consumed by our own problems that we can't see the pain of those around us. Take care of the needs of your family, to be sure, but don't forget about your neighbors.

BE A FRIEND TO WIDOWS

Diana lost her husband, John, several years ago. These are her suggestions for helping someone deal with such a loss:

1. Be a friend who says, *I want to power wash your siding*, instead of saying, *Call me if you need help.*

2. Be a friend who wants to hear me talk about the one I lost.

3. Be a friend who says, *I'll listen to anything you need to say, no matter how hard it is or how angry it sounds. You are safe with me.*

4. Be a friend who realizes there are no right words that will take away my pain. Just be with me.

people and laid his hands on the sick. Jesus blessed the children by laying hands on them (Matthew 19:14–15). Later we find it is a rite used to affirm a special calling (see Acts 13:1–3).

Administrative problems were solved, and now the gospel began to spread. Acts is careful to point out that priests came to faith in Christ (6:7). Who could these priests have been? It may have been righteous men like Zechariah (Luke 1:5–6) who were open to God's truth.[7] The selection of the seven made possible the multiplication of the ministry.

Love One Another (11:27–30)

At this point in history, Jews were living in a Greco-Roman world. The Greek way of life was prominent, but the Romans gained control before the birth of Christ. You will recognize the names of Roman emperors. Augustus Caesar (31 B.C—A.D. 14) was ruler at the time of Jesus' birth. Caesar instituted *Pax Romana* or *Roman Peace*. This concept enabled the spread of Christianity in the first century. Tiberius ruled A.D. 14–37. Caligula's disgraceful reign was A.D. 37–41. He promoted emperor worship. Claudius was ruler A.D. 41–54. During this time, the kingdom once again enjoyed peace. During A.D. 54–68, Christians were persecuted under the vile leadership of Nero.[8] Today's focal text mentions a famine during the reign of Claudius. Jewish historian Josephus provides confirmation, indicating the famine caused great distress throughout the land.[9]

In this passage, we learn of the prophecy of Agabus. A prophet was authorized to speak on behalf of another. Thus prophets of God spoke to people on God's behalf. They were given messages by the Spirit. This is not the only recorded prophecy of Agabus. In Acts 21:10–11, Agabus warned Paul about what would happen when he arrived in Jerusalem.

The role of the prophet was to provide guidance. We could spend a great deal of time discussing whether there are modern-day prophets. Whatever the result of the discussion, we can rest assured that God still provides guidance through his word, his Spirit, and his people. "With or without prophets, God directs us when we commit our lives to Him."[10]

Acts 11:29 states, "The disciples determined that according to their ability, each would send relief to the believers living in Judea." Consider how this might be done today through ministries such as disaster relief. It's true there are many needs today; recovery in Haiti and Japan, wildfires in Texas, damage from the floods and tornadoes in the Midwest and Southeast, hurricane relief. The needs are great. Yet, God has put us in this place at this time. Will we be found faithful in meeting the needs of those in our own congregation, as well as our brothers and sisters around the world?

Look at the remarkable chain of events. Through the missionary efforts of the Jerusalem church, the church of Antioch was birthed. The church at Antioch reached countless Gentiles and became the hub

GIFTS FROM THANKFUL HEARTS

One year, I was in Bulgaria during a holiday much like our Thanksgiving. I experienced the most amazing ministry. As a way to express thankfulness to God, Christians would cook food during the morning and evening worship services. At the beginning of the evening worship service, Christians would lay their gifts of food on the altar. After the service, the poor and needy were invited to the altar to take whatever food they wanted. What could we do to express our thankfulness to God and help someone in need?

for the entire mission enterprise of the first-century church. Then the church at Antioch would reach out to help their mother church.

Applying This Lesson to Life

Why did Luke interrupt his narrative by describing a routine administrative problem? I believe he wanted to emphasize that caring for each other is important. How can we hope to reach beyond our own congregation if we fail to minister to our brothers and sisters?

In addition, for a church to minister effectively, everyone must take responsibility. As Baptists, we believe in the priesthood of all believers. Ministry is at the core of our Christian discipleship. Our churches should model this biblical example of shared leadership, with clergy and lay leaders working in concert for the benefit of the body.

QUESTIONS

1. In Acts 6, the party with a grievance went directly to the leaders in charge. How do you respond when you are upset with something in the church?

2. What leadership lessons could we glean from how the apostles handled the crisis?

3. What qualities should we look for when selecting leaders in the congregation?

4. Consider needs within your congregation and beyond. What could your small group do to meet needs and share Christ?

5. What can be done to build stronger relationships with fellow Christians in other nations so as to be of greater help when situations of extreme need occur?

NOTES ───────────────────────────────────────

1. Unless otherwise indicated, all Scripture quotations in "Introducing the Book of Acts: Time to Act on Acts 1:8" and lessons 5 and 9 are taken from the New Revised Standard Version.

2. John B. Polhill, *Acts,* The New American Commentary, vol. 26 (Nashville, Tennessee: Broadman Press, 1992), 179.

3. Polhill, 180.

4. F.F. Bruce, *The Book of the Acts,* The New International Commentary on the New Testament, revised edition (Grand Rapids, Michigan: WM B Eerdmans Publishing Company, 1988), 121.

5. Bruce, 121.

6. Polhill, 182.

7. Bruce, 123.

8. H.I. Hester, *The Heart of the New Testament* (Nashville, Tennessee: Broadman Press, 1981), 45.

9. Josephus, *The Works of Josephus,* new updated edition (Peabody, Massachusetts: Hendrickson Publishers, 1988), 101.

10. Lawrence O. Richards, *Expository Dictionary of Bible Words* (Grand Rapids, Michigan: Zondervan Publishing House, 1991), 508.

11. Ralph Martin, *New Testament Foundations: A Guide for Students,* volume 1 (Grand Rapids, Michigan: WM B Eerdmans Publishing Company, 1975), 53–54.

12. Martin, 55.

13. Martin, 54–55.

FOCAL TEXT
Acts 6:8—7:5, 9–28,
35–41, 44–60

BACKGROUND
Acts 6:8—7:60

MAIN IDEA
Stephen challenged accepted
views and practices as
he proclaimed Jesus.

QUESTION TO EXPLORE
What accepted views and
practices are keeping us from
communicating the message
of Jesus to all people?

STUDY AIM
To identify views and
practices that may be
keeping me from being
Jesus' witness to all people

QUICK READ
When the worst happened
and Stephen was arrested and
killed, God was at his best,
taking the blood of the first
Christian martyr and making
it the seed of the church. The
followers of Jesus thrust out
by the persecution took the
good news of Jesus Christ
to the ends of the earth.

LESSON SIX
Challenge Accepted Views for Jesus' Sake

"When you are bumped, you will spill whatever fills you!" Jack Gray, one of my seminary professors, captured our attention with that statement.

All of us are bumped from time to time. What comes out? Stephen was arrested and martyred by the early opponents of Christianity. But when they bumped him, this great man of God, full of the Spirit, God's grace, and God's power, spilled forth the truth and love of God.

Stephen was not one of the Twelve. In fact, when the church replaced Judas Iscariot, Stephen did not make the short list of the candidates for twelfth apostle (Acts 1:23). We learn prior to Acts 7 that Stephen was chosen by the church to serve when they were facing a crisis in the food distribution to the widows (6:1–7; lesson 5). To deal with the crisis, the apostles proposed to the congregation that seven be selected from among them and "to turn this responsibility over to them" (6:3).

Stephen stood at the top of the list of the seven servants. Stephen was "full of faith and of the Holy Spirit" (6:5). After he and his partners apparently resolved the dispute, "the word of God spread," and "the number of disciples in Jerusalem increased rapidly" (6:7). But Stephen's work had just begun.[1]

ACTS 6:8–15

[8] Now Stephen, a man full of God's grace and power, performed great wonders and signs among the people. [9] Opposition arose, however, from members of the Synagogue of the Freedmen (as it was called)—Jews of Cyrene and Alexandria as well as the provinces of Cilicia and Asia—who began to argue with Stephen. [10] But they could not stand up against the wisdom the Spirit gave him as he spoke.

[11] Then they secretly persuaded some men to say, "We have heard Stephen speak blasphemous words against Moses and against God."

[12] So they stirred up the people and the elders and the teachers of the law. They seized Stephen and brought him before the Sanhedrin. [13] They produced false witnesses, who testified, "This fellow never stops speaking against this holy place and against the law. [14] For we have heard him say that this Jesus of Nazareth will

destroy this place and change the customs Moses handed down to us."

¹⁵ All who were sitting in the Sanhedrin looked intently at Stephen, and they saw that his face was like the face of an angel.

ACTS 7:1–5, 9–28, 35–41, 44–60

¹ Then the high priest asked Stephen, "Are these charges true?"

² To this he replied: "Brothers and fathers, listen to me! The God of glory appeared to our father Abraham while he was still in Mesopotamia, before he lived in Harran. ³ 'Leave your country and your people,' God said, 'and go to the land I will show you.'

⁴ "So he left the land of the Chaldeans and settled in Harran. After the death of his father, God sent him to this land where you are now living. ⁵ He gave him no inheritance here, not even enough ground to set his foot on. But God promised him that he and his descendants after him would possess the land, even though at that time Abraham had no child.

• •

⁹ "Because the patriarchs were jealous of Joseph, they sold him as a slave into Egypt. But God was with him ¹⁰ and rescued him from all his troubles. He gave Joseph wisdom and enabled him to gain the goodwill of Pharaoh king of Egypt. So Pharaoh made him ruler over Egypt and all his palace.

¹¹ "Then a famine struck all Egypt and Canaan, bringing great suffering, and our ancestors could not find food. ¹² When Jacob heard that there was grain in Egypt, he sent our forefathers on their first visit. ¹³ On their second visit, Joseph told his brothers who he was, and Pharaoh learned about Joseph's family. ¹⁴ After this, Joseph sent for his father Jacob and his whole family, seventy-five in all. ¹⁵ Then Jacob went down to Egypt, where he and our ancestors died. ¹⁶ Their bodies were brought back to Shechem and placed in the tomb that Abraham had bought from the sons of Hamor at Shechem for a certain sum of money.

¹⁷ "As the time drew near for God to fulfill his promise to

Abraham, the number of our people in Egypt had greatly increased. [18] Then 'a new king, to whom Joseph meant nothing, came to power in Egypt.' [19] He dealt treacherously with our people and oppressed our ancestors by forcing them to throw out their newborn babies so that they would die.

[20] "At that time Moses was born, and he was no ordinary child. For three months he was cared for by his family. [21] When he was placed outside, Pharaoh's daughter took him and brought him up as her own son. [22] Moses was educated in all the wisdom of the Egyptians and was powerful in speech and action.

[23] "When Moses was forty years old, he decided to visit his own people, the Israelites. [24] He saw one of them being mistreated by an Egyptian, so he went to his defense and avenged him by killing the Egyptian. [25] Moses thought that his own people would realize that God was using him to rescue them, but they did not. [26] The next day Moses came upon two Israelites who were fighting. He tried to reconcile them by saying, 'Men, you are brothers; why do you want to hurt each other?'

[27] "But the man who was mistreating the other pushed Moses aside and said, 'Who made you ruler and judge over us? [28] Are you thinking of killing me as you killed the Egyptian yesterday?'

• •

[35] "This is the same Moses they had rejected with the words, 'Who made you ruler and judge?' He was sent to be their ruler and deliverer by God himself, through the angel who appeared to him in the bush. [36] He led them out of Egypt and performed wonders and signs in Egypt, at the Red Sea and for forty years in the wilderness.

[37] "This is the Moses who told the Israelites, 'God will raise up for you a prophet like me from your own people.' [38] He was in the assembly in the wilderness, with the angel who spoke to him on Mount Sinai, and with our ancestors; and he received living words to pass on to us.

[39] "But our ancestors refused to obey him. Instead, they rejected him and in their hearts turned back to Egypt. [40] They told Aaron, 'Make us gods who will go before us. As for this fellow Moses who

led us out of Egypt—we don't know what has happened to him!' ⁴¹ That was the time they made an idol in the form of a calf. They brought sacrifices to it and reveled in what their own hands had made.

• •

⁴⁴ "Our ancestors had the tabernacle of the covenant law with them in the wilderness. It had been made as God directed Moses, according to the pattern he had seen. ⁴⁵ After receiving the tabernacle, our ancestors under Joshua brought it with them when they took the land from the nations God drove out before them. It remained in the land until the time of David, ⁴⁶ who enjoyed God's favor and asked that he might provide a dwelling place for the God of Jacob. ⁴⁷ But it was Solomon who built a house for him.

⁴⁸ "However, the Most High does not live in houses made by human hands. As the prophet says:
⁴⁹ "'Heaven is my throne,
    and the earth is my footstool.
What kind of house will you build for me?
    says the Lord.
Or where will my resting place be?
⁵⁰ Has not my hand made all these things?'

⁵¹ "You stiff-necked people! Your hearts and ears are still uncircumcised. You are just like your ancestors: You always resist the Holy Spirit! ⁵² Was there ever a prophet your ancestors did not persecute? They even killed those who predicted the coming of the Righteous One. And now you have betrayed and murdered him—⁵³ you who have received the law that was given through angels but have not obeyed it."

⁵⁴ When the members of the Sanhedrin heard this, they were furious and gnashed their teeth at him. ⁵⁵ But Stephen, full of the Holy Spirit, looked up to heaven and saw the glory of God, and Jesus standing at the right hand of God. ⁵⁶ "Look," he said, "I see heaven open and the Son of Man standing at the right hand of God."

⁵⁷ At this they covered their ears and, yelling at the top of their

voices, they all rushed at him, [58] dragged him out of the city and began to stone him. Meanwhile, the witnesses laid their coats at the feet of a young man named Saul.

[59] While they were stoning him, Stephen prayed, "Lord Jesus, receive my spirit." [60] Then he fell on his knees and cried out, "Lord, do not hold this sin against them." When he had said this, he fell asleep.

An Irrefutable Witness (6:8—7:5, 9–28, 35–41, 44–53)

Stephen, "a man full of God's grace and power, did great wonders and miraculous signs among the people" (6:8). As he did, he was arrested by his adversaries. They had quarreled with him about the work of God. Gifted in apologetics, or defending the faith, Stephen had testified of Christ and confounded his opponents with his words. When they could not stand it any longer and they could not stop him, Stephen's opponents arrested him. Falsely accusing him of speaking against the temple and the law, they put him on trial before the high priest. There, Stephen, with the countenance of an angel, answered his adversaries. When we take a stand for Christ, no opponent will be able to stand against us.

STEPHEN

Was Stephen a deacon? In Luke's description of the selection of the seven in Acts 6, he did not use the word deacon. Often we equate this group in Acts 6 with the office of deacon that Paul described in the pastoral letters (see 1 Timothy 3).

Stephen and Philip manifested wonderful gifts. Stephen was a gifted apologist or defender of the faith. Later Philip demonstrated a gift in evangelism.

To say that a deacon is a servant in the church is not to say that this person is limited in being gifted. Some of our most gifted leaders in the church are the so-called lay leaders, gifted by God to help advance the work of the gospel in our world today.

As we read this lengthy message, it may seem that Stephen's story of God's work among his people is difficult to follow. As he taught them, though, Stephen showed how the movement of God led his people to move. For example, Abraham left the land of the Chaldeans (7:4). Moses later left the desert to go into Egypt (7:30–38). When God moves, so should we. Stephen's recalcitrant hearers stubbornly resisted any movement of God. They had decided to focus on the law and the temple more than they focused on the Lord their God. Their motto might be summarized with the words, *Come weal, come woe, our status is quo.*

Similarly, Moses often found God's people immovable (7:39). They mumbled, grumbled, and resisted the work of God through Moses steadfastly. Stephen shows us both by his exhortation and his example that God's work in the world has always faced opposition.

Stephen had been accused of attacking the temple and the law (6:11–14). So he answered their accusations by showing that Moses, who gave the law, faced opposition as well. Then Solomon built the temple, which Stephen's detractors sought to defend from him (7:47). But even the people of Solomon's day knew that the heavens could not contain and constrain the God of heaven and earth, much less a building erected by human hands (7:48–50).

At any point, Stephen might have stopped and compromised with his opponents. But in the end he left them with an irrefutable witness to the work of God. He reminded them that their fathers had killed the prophets (7:51–53). Following in their fathers' footsteps, they had betrayed and murdered the Righteous One, Jesus the Messiah. In the name of loving the law, many of the generations before had rejected the words God spoke to them through the prophets.

Even in our day, some choose legalism over love. Have you ever known someone who claimed to love the Bible but failed to live it? When we bear witness to the truth by telling the story of God's love revealed through Jesus Christ, our message is irrefutable.

An Incarnational and Sacrificial Witness (7:54–60)

Stephen loved the Lord first and best. His death reminds us of Jesus' death in two ways. Like Jesus in the Garden of Gethsemane, Stephen fell to his knees in prayer. Then Stephen forgave his murderers just as Jesus

APPLYING THIS SCRIPTURE

To apply this Scripture in your daily walk:

- Find those who need to hear the story of the gospel. They are all around us.
- Write out a brief story of the gospel of Jesus Christ.
- Prepare a story of how God has worked in your life to help you become a believer.
- Practice sharing these stories with friends.
- Ask God to help you to share the good news of Christ's transforming power with others.
- Speak up for Christ and challenge the view that people are saved by doing good works.

did, praying, "Lord, do not hold this sin against them" (7:60; see Luke 23:34). So his last words were about Jesus.

As the crowd prepared to stone Stephen to death, he lifted his eyes heavenward and saw Jesus standing at the right hand of God. We often hear in Scripture about Jesus seated at the right hand of the Father. Why would Jesus stand on this occasion? My New Testament Greek teacher Dr. James Brooks suggested in our seminary class, "Undoubtedly Jesus was standing in honor of this servant who honored him in life and also in his death."

The poet Alfred, Lord Tennyson (1809–1892) wrote about Stephen:[2]

> He heeded not reviling tones
> Nor sold his heart to idle moans,
> Tho cursed and scorned and bruised with stones
> But looking upward full of grace
> He prayed and from a happy place
> God's glory smote him on the face.

In addition to Stephen, Saul was there. Rabbi Gamaliel's star student Saul supervised the coat closet while the mob stoned Stephen to death. In Acts 8 we learn that Saul began at this point to persecute the church in earnest (8:1–3; 9:1–3). Many followers of Christ were forced out of

Jerusalem in these days (8:2). But God's purpose was not thwarted. When the worst of the world are at their worst, our God is at his best. God used the very persecution that seemed to threaten the life of the church to empower his people to have the audacity to share the gospel of Jesus Christ with even greater boldness.

In the charter of the church's mission, Jesus had said in Acts 1:8, "You will be my witnesses in Jerusalem, and in all Judea and Samaria, and to the ends of the earth." Soon, Acts will show us Philip taking the gospel to the Samaritans (8:4–7). So many of these who had been despised before now received Christ as Savior and Lord. Then, led by the Spirit, Philip visited a desert road and baptized an Ethiopian eunuch (8:26–40; see lesson 7). Later, nameless disciples from Cyrene and Cyprus, forced out of Jerusalem by the persecution, stopped in Antioch and shared Christ with the Greeks also (11:19–21; see lesson 9). There in Antioch God built the next great church of the first century after Jerusalem. There the believers were identified with Christ by being the first to be called Christians. By this time Saul had come to Christ on the road to Damascus (Acts 9:1–19; see lesson 8), and he became one of the leaders at Antioch. This prompted the church father Augustine (354–430) to say, "The church owed Paul to the prayer of Stephen." By the end of the Book of Acts, Paul was preaching the gospel in Rome, nearer still "to the ends of the earth" (1:8).

Implications and Actions

As Jesus showed us incarnational ministry by becoming flesh and entering our world, so the church must become an incarnational witness going into the world. Stephen was not a pastor, but he was a gifted leader in the early church. Are we waiting for the ministers to reach the world? What barriers stop us from reaching the nations with the good news of Jesus Christ?

Legalism leads us to keep score, but love leads us to life. As Christ fills our lives, we are prepared to take a stand for him. Because we have been forgiven, we are able through Christ to forgive others who have harmed us. Christ's love in us helps others to trust in him as well.

This is not the time for us to say to the world around us, *Come and see.* This is the time to *go and tell.* As you go, be a disciple of Jesus Christ, and make disciples of Jesus Christ.

We can either lower our eyes in despair and say, *Look what the world has come to.* Or we can lift our eyes in delight and say, *Look who has come to the world!*

QUESTIONS

1. How did Stephen confront the false assumptions of those who questioned him?

2. Stephen's accusers sought to protect the law and the temple. What do legalists in our churches today seek to protect?

3. Why do you think Jesus was standing instead of sitting at the right hand of God?

4. How was Stephen like Jesus in his death?

5. Are you willing to forgive those who have harmed you? What will happen to them if you do? if you don't? What will happen to *you* if you forgive?

6. How does the church owe Saul's conversion to Stephen's prayer?

NOTES

1. Unless otherwise indicated, all Scripture quotations in lessons 3–4, 6–8, 10–13 are taken from The Holy Bible, New International Version (North American Edition), copyright © 1973, 1978, 1984 by the International Bible Society.

2. Alfred, Lord Tennyson, "The Two Voices," stanzas 68–75.

FOCAL TEXT
Acts 8:26–40

BACKGROUND
Acts 8:4–40

MAIN IDEA
Responding to the leading
of the Spirit, Philip told
the inquirer the good
news about Jesus.

QUESTION TO EXPLORE
How can we be more
sensitive and responsive to
the leading of God's Spirit
in sharing the gospel?

STUDY AIM
To identify ways to be
more responsive to the
leading of God's Spirit
in sharing the gospel

QUICK READ
Philip's sensitivity to the
leadership of the Holy Spirit
provided an opportunity to
share the good news of Jesus
with a person who would
normally be excluded. God
used Philip to include an
outsider in God's kingdom.

LESSON SEVEN
Be Available to God's Spirit to Share the Gospel

Amazing things happen. An undocumented immigrant came across the Rio Grande several years ago looking for work. While he was here, he heard the message of Jesus as one of our Texas Baptist churches ministered to him. He accepted the Lord and grew in his faith, but eventually he had to go back to Mexico. He came from a part of Mexico that had been identified as an unreached people group. When he got back to his home in Mexico, he started a church there and became the pastor. Now there is a thriving church in a place where there was no church before because someone in South Texas was determined to be sensitive to the leadership of God's Spirit in sharing the gospel.

Consider the similarities of that story to this lesson's Scripture passage.[1]

ACTS 8:26–40

26 Now an angel of the Lord said to Philip, "Go south to the road—the desert road—that goes down from Jerusalem to Gaza." 27 So he started out, and on his way he met an Ethiopian eunuch, an important official in charge of all the treasury of the Kandake (which means "queen of the Ethiopians"). This man had gone to Jerusalem to worship, 28 and on his way home was sitting in his chariot reading the Book of Isaiah the prophet. 29 The Spirit told Philip, "Go to that chariot and stay near it."

30 Then Philip ran up to the chariot and heard the man reading Isaiah the prophet. "Do you understand what you are reading?" Philip asked.

31 "How can I," he said, "unless someone explains it to me?" So he invited Philip to come up and sit with him.

32 This is the passage of Scripture the eunuch was reading:

"He was led like a sheep to the slaughter,
    and as a lamb before its shearer is silent,
    so he did not open his mouth.
33 In his humiliation he was deprived of justice.
    Who can speak of his descendants?
    For his life was taken from the earth."

34 The eunuch asked Philip, "Tell me, please, who is the prophet talking about, himself or someone else?" 35 Then Philip began with

that very passage of Scripture and told him the good news about Jesus.

36 As they traveled along the road, they came to some water and the eunuch said, "Look, here is water. What can stand in the way of my being baptized?" [37] 38 And he gave orders to stop the chariot. Then both Philip and the eunuch went down into the water and Philip baptized him. 39 When they came up out of the water, the Spirit of the Lord suddenly took Philip away, and the eunuch did not see him again, but went on his way rejoicing. 40 Philip, however, appeared at Azotus and traveled about, preaching the gospel in all the towns until he reached Caesarea.

People Need to Know About Jesus

Philip was one of the seven men elected by the church in Jerusalem to minister to the church's Greek-speaking widows "in the daily distribution of food" (Acts 6:1; see lesson 5). Sometimes people confuse Philip with one of the twelve original disciples. He was not one of the Twelve, but there is no doubt he was an early follower of Jesus. After Philip's election by the church, the Spirit directed Philip to go beyond his duties of serving the poor. The Spirit moved him to share the gospel with others.

Sharing the gospel is not a new-fangled program thought up by a denominational agency. Telling people about Jesus saturates the pages of the New Testament. The Holy Spirit continues to move in believers today, motivating us to share the good news of Jesus with others.

Philip was no stranger to telling people about Jesus. Philip had been busy in the suspicious realm of the Samaritans for some time (8:4–25). Jesus had told his followers before he ascended that they would be witnesses in Samaria. But Jesus also told them they were to be witnesses beyond Judea and Samaria to the rest of the world (1:8). The Holy Spirit had already impressed on Philip that all people everywhere needed to know about Jesus, regardless of their social acceptability. So, when the Spirit spoke to Philip again, he was ready to go.

One day the Spirit of the Lord told Philip to go out on the desert road leading to the town of Gaza. He obeyed, and when he arrived he saw a chariot passing by with a man reading the prophet Isaiah out loud. Philip ran up to the chariot and asked the man (8:30), "Do you understand what you are reading?"

The man turned out to be an Ethiopian eunuch, a high government official for his country down in Africa. He was probably what was called a God-fearer—a person who was interested in the worship of the one true God, but who was not a Jew.

How can I understand what I am reading unless someone explains it to me? he asked (8:31). Philip took this as a great opportunity from God. He jumped up in the chariot, and Philip could see that the man was reading from the Old Testament prophet Isaiah: "He was led as a sheep to the slaughter, and as a lamb before its shearer is silent, so he did not open his mouth" (Acts 8:32; see Isaiah 53:7).

Who is he talking about? the eunuch wanted to know. Starting from there, Philip told this man about Jesus. The man heard the gospel and believed it because Philip was sensitive and responsive to the leading of God's Spirit.

The Spirit Leads Beyond Our Boundaries

The Holy Spirit led Philip to burst through human boundaries to share the gospel. Such a thought was revolutionary to Jewish Christians in Philip's day. Preaching to the Samaritans was already out of the box, but to share with this Ethiopian eunuch was unthinkable. But because Philip was sensitive to the leadership of the Spirit, he was willing to do anything God asked him to do.

The gospel of Jesus Christ goes beyond all boundaries. It transcends boundaries of nations, prejudice, and social and religious status to give good news to everyone.

Boundaries are a hot topic in America these days. Border security and illegal immigration are huge concerns in a world of terror and economic distress. Perhaps it is true that for national interests and safety, politicians and society need to address this issue in some humane way. But when we are talking about Jesus, national boundaries are of little consequence.

For example, this Ethiopian eunuch was not a Jew but a Gentile, and an African Gentile at that! In Judaism at that time, there was nothing

ETHIOPIA

Ethiopia in biblical times was not the same as the modern country of Ethiopia. Modern Ethiopia lies southeast of Sudan and west of Somalia. In the New Testament era, Ethiopia was farther north along the Nile River, just to the south of Egypt.

Before New Testament times Egypt and Ethiopia were closely related. For a while Egypt controlled Ethiopia, and then Ethiopians controlled Egypt. By the time Philip met the Ethiopian eunuch, Ethiopia was a smaller country ruled by a series of queens who bore the title *candace*. *Candace* is a title rather than a personal name. The eunuch in the story was a high government official for the queen.

Tradition says the Ethiopian went home and shared the gospel there. It is possible that this was the beginning of the Coptic Christian movement that is still alive today in Egypt.

more despicable than a Gentile. But Philip didn't care about that. The Spirit had convinced him that everybody, everywhere ought to know about Jesus.

On top of that, this person was a eunuch. The Jewish law said that a eunuch could never become a Jew, and in fact could not even enter the temple. Deuteronomy 23:1 says, "No one who has been emasculated by crushing or cutting may enter the assembly of the LORD." There was no room for an African Gentile eunuch in the Jewish faith. The best he could hope for was just to learn about God but never really know God.

We still have a tendency to predetermine who is eligible for salvation. Culture, religious beliefs, and personal scruples form boundaries that separate us from some people. But the New Testament is very clear: the Holy Spirit knows no boundaries.

In the gospel of Jesus Christ there is room for everyone. Everybody is invited to sit at the table of the Lord. It doesn't matter whether you are black or white; rich or poor; Mexican, Chinese, or Irish. The Holy Spirit leads us to share the gospel beyond our boundaries because everyone needs to know Jesus. This strange man from a strange place came to know Jesus because Philip followed the leadership of the Spirit to share the good news with him.

Baptism Is the Proper Response to Belief

Accepting the good news about Jesus is not the end of the Christian life. There are things to do after we come to Christ. The Ethiopian recognized that the decision he made to follow Jesus was just the beginning of a new life, not the end.

The first step in following Jesus is to be baptized. Baptism does not literally wash our sins away, and neither is it necessary for salvation. But it is inconceivable that a person who has decided to follow Jesus would not want to be baptized. If a person cannot take even this first step of obedience how can the person be serious about following the Lord? Presumably, Philip had discussed baptism with the man in their conversation.

When Philip and the Ethiopian came to a body of water, the Ethiopian asked (Acts 8:37), "Why shouldn't I be baptized?" Literally the question was, *What prevents me from being baptized?* The word translated *prevent* is a rare word in the Bible. It means *to hinder or to keep from.*

In Jewish life a Gentile became a Jew by being baptized and circumcised. Because the man was a eunuch, circumcision was out of the question, considering the barrier of the law. Therefore, baptism into Judaism was also prevented.

DISCERNING THE PROMPTING OF THE HOLY SPIRIT

1. Be busy in the Lord's work. Philip was already doing God's work when he heard the Spirit.
2. Be sensitive to opportunities to share your faith. The Spirit may have arranged that opportunity.
3. Study the Scriptures. The Spirit speaks through the witness of the Bible.
4. Be willing to overcome social and cultural barriers to share the gospel with people.
5. Always be ready for another assignment from God.

But the good news of Jesus removes all barriers. Since the man had become a follower of Jesus, there was nothing to prevent this man from being baptized. The Holy Spirit led Philip to the radical conclusion that there was nothing to stop this man from full fellowship with God and with other believers. Therefore, there was nothing to prevent him from being baptized.

Baptists believe the Bible indicates baptism is for believers. Lack of faith is the only barrier to being baptized. Nowhere does the New Testament provide an example of people being baptized in the name of Jesus before they come to conscious faith in Christ. Furthermore, the New Testament indicates baptism was by immersion. The word *baptize* means *to dip or immerse.* Immersion of a believer symbolizes the death and burial of the old person and the resurrection of a new person who now lives for Christ. Baptism is a vow to God and a witness to others that we will follow Jesus for the rest of our lives. That was the case with this Ethiopian.

The Spirit Moves New Believers to Share

Look what happened in the story about Philip and the Ethiopian. After the Ethiopian accepted Christ and was baptized, the Bible says that the Spirit "snatched Philip away" (8:39, NASB, NRSV), freeing him to share the good news in other places. The Spirit was not finished working through Philip, and Philip was not finished with responding to the Spirit's leadership.

The Ethiopian "went on his way rejoicing" (8:40). Of course he was rejoicing. He had found out who Jesus was. When you truly find out personally that Jesus is the One whom the prophets foretold, the One who suffered and died for our sins, the One who rose from the grave, the One who now gives eternal life, you can't help but rejoice. The eunuch rejoiced all the way back to Ethiopia. In fact, he never stopped rejoicing because he had found out who Jesus is.

We don't know for sure, but there is a tradition that this man went home and told the people at home about the gospel of Jesus Christ. You know why he did that? Because when he came to know Christ, the Spirit moved in him as well, and he responded to that leadership.

Implications and Actions

The command from Jesus to be witnesses to Judea, Samaria, and to the ends of the earth (1:8) has not changed. Neither has the prompting of the Holy Spirit in the lives of believers changed. The Holy Spirit still speaks and still provides opportunities to share the good news about Jesus with all kinds of people.

Sometimes the Spirit tells us to share the gospel with people around us, people who are like us. But the Spirit still prompts us to cross cultural, social, and even religious barriers to share the good news of Jesus with people who are very different from us. That is not always easy. There are people in this world who make us very uncomfortable. We question their way of life, their morals, and their personal habits, and we tend to shy away from any kind of contact. But the Spirit who prompted Philip to share with the Ethiopian eunuch is the same Spirit who lives in us today.

Read the Scriptures. Listen to the Spirit. Go out into the world under the power and leadership of God's Holy Spirit, and share the good news about Jesus.

QUESTIONS

1. Make a list of the kinds of people outside your normal social interaction. What can you, your class, or your church do to communicate the gospel to them?

2. Do you think Philip had any misgivings about getting into the chariot with the Ethiopian eunuch given the religious restrictions of Jewish people? Why or why not?

3. Philip explained Scripture to the Ethiopian when he was talking with him. How can Scripture help when sharing the good news about Jesus?

4. What is the meaning of baptism? Why do Baptists practice believer's baptism by immersion?

5. How do you know when the Holy Spirit is prompting you to do something?

NOTES

1. Unless otherwise indicated, all Scripture quotations in lessons 3–4, 6–8, 10–13 are taken from The Holy Bible, New International Version (North American Edition), copyright © 1973, 1978, 1984 by the International Bible Society.

FOCAL TEXT
Acts 9:1–22, 26–28

BACKGROUND
Acts 9:1–28

MAIN IDEA
Paul, Christianity's
greatest enemy, became
the greatest missionary
for Christ, with help from
Ananias and Barnabas.

QUESTION TO EXPLORE
Who's the most unlikely
person to become a Christian
whom you know personally?

STUDY AIM
To identify how God can
use me to reach an unlikely
person for Christ

QUICK READ
Paul's conversion experience
teaches us how God can use
ordinary people to reach
someone who was the most
unlikely person to become
a Christian and, indeed, a
Christian missionary.

LESSON EIGHT
Don't Neglect the Hard Cases

Whoever introduced the concept of *opposites attract* probably did not have the Apostle Paul in mind. Paul and Jesus Christ were on totally opposite ends of the spectrum. Paul having a relationship with Jesus Christ was totally opposite of what he had embraced as his life calling. This made Paul the most unlikely person to become a Christian.

Is there someone in your life whom you feel is unlikely to be reached by the gospel of Jesus Christ? We sometimes categorize such people as *hard cases.* However, like Ananias and Barnabas, God wants to use you to witness to them. We must never underestimate the power of God to reach someone we have deemed unreachable.[1]

ACTS 9:1–22, 26–28

[1] Meanwhile, Saul was still breathing out murderous threats against the Lord's disciples. He went to the high priest [2] and asked him for letters to the synagogues in Damascus, so that if he found any there who belonged to the Way, whether men or women, he might take them as prisoners to Jerusalem. [3] As he neared Damascus on his journey, suddenly a light from heaven flashed around him. [4] He fell to the ground and heard a voice say to him, "Saul, Saul, why do you persecute me?"

[5] "Who are you, Lord?" Saul asked.

"I am Jesus, whom you are persecuting," he replied. [6] "Now get up and go into the city, and you will be told what you must do."

[7] The men traveling with Saul stood there speechless; they heard the sound but did not see anyone. [8] Saul got up from the ground, but when he opened his eyes he could see nothing. So they led him by the hand into Damascus. [9] For three days he was blind, and did not eat or drink anything.

[10] In Damascus there was a disciple named Ananias. The Lord called to him in a vision, "Ananias!"

"Yes, Lord," he answered.

[11] The Lord told him, "Go to the house of Judas on Straight Street and ask for a man from Tarsus named Saul, for he is praying. [12] In a vision he has seen a man named Ananias come and place his hands on him to restore his sight."

¹³ "Lord," Ananias answered, "I have heard many reports about this man and all the harm he has done to your holy people in Jerusalem. ¹⁴ And he has come here with authority from the chief priests to arrest all who call on your name."

¹⁵ But the Lord said to Ananias, "Go! This man is my chosen instrument to proclaim my name to the Gentiles and their kings and to the people of Israel. ¹⁶ I will show him how much he must suffer for my name."

¹⁷ Then Ananias went to the house and entered it. Placing his hands on Saul, he said, "Brother Saul, the Lord—Jesus, who appeared to you on the road as you were coming here—has sent me so that you may see again and be filled with the Holy Spirit." ¹⁸ Immediately, something like scales fell from Saul's eyes, and he could see again. He got up and was baptized, ¹⁹ and after taking some food, he regained his strength.

Saul spent several days with the disciples in Damascus. ²⁰ At once he began to preach in the synagogues that Jesus is the Son of God. ²¹ All those who heard him were astonished and asked, "Isn't he the man who raised havoc in Jerusalem among those who call on this name? And hasn't he come here to take them as prisoners to the chief priests?" ²² Yet Saul grew more and more powerful and baffled the Jews living in Damascus by proving that Jesus is the Messiah.

• •

²⁶ When he came to Jerusalem, he tried to join the disciples, but they were all afraid of him, not believing that he really was a disciple. ²⁷ But Barnabas took him and brought him to the apostles. He told them how Saul on his journey had seen the Lord and that the Lord had spoken to him, and how in Damascus he had preached fearlessly in the name of Jesus. ²⁸ So Saul stayed with them and moved about freely in Jerusalem, speaking boldly in the name of the Lord.

The Miracle of Paul's Conversion (9:1–8)

Our first introduction to Paul is in Acts 7:58 where he was a consenting witness to the stoning of Stephen. He is described there as "a young man named Saul." The Greek word rendered "young man" would have been used to describe a man in his early to late twenties. His consenting to Stephen's martyrdom is mentioned in Acts 8:1.

By the time we reach Acts 9, Paul had become notorious for his acts of persecution toward the church. Word had spread to the believers throughout the regions of Judea and Samaria and on to Damascus that Paul was a force to be feared. He was going from town to town arresting the followers of Christ and had the authority to do so. Jewish communities in and around Palestine had great respect for the high priest. Therefore letters to the synagogue leaders commending Paul's mission were taken very seriously and were accompanied by full cooperation.

Paul viewed his mission of persecuting Christians as his way of lending assistance to the will of God. Paul was steeped in Judaism, which gave him the fuel to eradicate anything that did not follow his Pharisaic teachings. Paul was insurmountably devout in his beliefs and his hatred of this new sect that Acts refers to as the followers of "the Way" (Acts 9:2). He testified before King Agrippa in Acts 26:5 how he conformed to "the strictest sect of our religion" and "lived as a Pharisee."

At the beginning of Acts 9 we see Paul and his entourage travelling to Damascus. Damascus is a city about 130 miles northeast of Jerusalem. A growing number of Jews lived in Damascus at the time of Paul's journey. The city contained thirty to forty synagogues during this time, each of them with specific instructions concerning Paul's mission and authority. This journey would have taken Paul and his companions approximately five or six days on foot.

The three accounts in Acts of Paul's conversion (9:1–19; 22:1–21; 26:12–18) indicate that Paul's encounter with Christ happened on the road before he reached Damascus. Acts 22 and 26 indicate it was about the noon hour. Acts may mention the time of Paul's encounter to highlight the fact that Paul and his companions were fully awake, with all of their cognitive faculties. This is to further strengthen Paul's later testimony as to not allow the experience to be dismissed as a dream or vision Paul would have had while sleeping.

CONVERSION EXPERIENCE

Paul's experience was memorable and points to a unique time in every believer's life. The reality of our personal salvation is impressed on us by some factual event or moment where Christ reveals himself to us through the Holy Spirit. These moments arrest our attention and shatter doubt that Christ's presence in our lives is real. In our Baptist tradition we refer to this as having a *conversion experience.*

Christ's encounter with Paul caught him completely by surprise. Suddenly a light shone and engulfed Paul. Acts 9:3 states that the light was "from heaven." Paul would not have known the origin of the light initially, only that it was from above. On seeing the light, Paul fell to the ground. The Greek word rendered "fell" (9:4) means *to fall down in a prostrate position.* This word is also used to describe prostrating oneself as an act of reverent worship of a deity. Paul, being a religious person, would have viewed this light as a divine sign from heaven. For Paul this was a life-changing event that he would never forget.

While Paul was lying prostrate, he "heard a voice say to him, 'Saul, Saul, why do you persecute me?'" (9:4). Notice here the use of the name "Saul" as opposed to *Paul.* Up until now Acts has used his Jewish name "Saul." Acts 13:9 identifies him as "Saul, who was also called Paul." Several questions abound as to why the name change and whether Christ changed his name or Paul changed it himself. We are not told specifically when, why, or how Paul's name was changed from Saul. One explanation for this would be that Paul was sent to preach the gospel to the Gentiles. There was strong hatred between Jews and Gentiles during the time of Paul's conversion. Having a Romanized name (Paul) would have made it easier for him to identify with his Gentile audience, thus allowing them to receive his message more readily.

The voice that Paul heard identified himself as the One whom Paul was persecuting. The true power of Paul's encounter with Jesus can be seen in that here is one who was a staunch enemy of the church being submissive to the One who reigns over the church. Those who position themselves against Christ and his teachings must be confronted by Christ himself. If we seek to reach those in opposition to our witness for Christ, we must continue to pray for those moments that Jesus Christ will reveal himself convincingly to those who deny his existence.

In verse 5, Paul used the Greek term *kyrios,* which is translated "Lord," to address Jesus, although Paul did not fully understand to whom he was speaking. This same word appears throughout the New Testament as the term assigned to Jesus, meaning *Master* or *Sovereign Messiah.* After Jesus identified himself as the One to whom Paul was speaking, Paul used the term "Lord" again (26:10). This time he used it as an act of submission to the call of Christ.

This experience had miraculously left Paul temporarily blind. He had to be led into the city by those who travelled with him. The blinding of Paul's eyes can be interpreted as a symbol of his spiritual blindness when confronted by *the Light of the world.* To this point Paul had physical sight, but he was living in darkness. No longer was he the zealot wielding an arrest warrant stalking the sheep of God's pasture. After one miraculous moment, Jesus had changed him into a humble servant awaiting his Master's instructions.

The Meaning of Paul's Conversion (9:9–19)

When Paul reached Damascus he was housed at the home of Judas (9:11). He continued fasting and praying for three days while waiting on instructions concerning his new assignment (9:9). The Lord commissioned a disciple of that city named Ananias to carry a message to Paul and minister to him.

Ananias, whose name means *whom God has graciously given,* obviously had a previous encounter with Jesus because of his recognition of Jesus' voice in a vision. It is interesting to note that Ananias's name relates directly to how the Lord used him to guide Paul. God chose Ananias not arbitrarily but specifically. Ananias had been spiritually prepared to be the one God would use to guide Paul to the truth of his calling. The Lord had *graciously given* Paul a trusted disciple who would aid him in receiving God's command.

God has prepared many of his servants to be used as guides for those who are still in darkness. We must pray and be ready whenever we are given the opportunity to witness for Christ to others.

Ananias received divine instructions with much anxiety. He was reluctant about this journey because of the fear that was prevalent among the Jewish Christians in Damascus concerning Saul of Tarsus, a persecutor of the followers of Jesus. The Lord compassionately responded to the fears of Ananias's heart by revealing Paul's new purpose. The Lord said to Ananias in verse 15, "Go! This man is my chosen instrument to proclaim my name before the Gentiles and their kings and before the people of Israel."

Paul had now gone from being a feared adversary of the church to a "chosen instrument" of God. The idea expressed through the use of the word "chosen" is represented here by the Greek word *ekloge,* which means *to be picked out.* The context of its use in verse 15 indicates that God in his sovereignty had already "chosen" Paul as a part of his divine will that was established before the foundation of the world. Paul would now assume his role as ambassador for Christ with the help of Ananias. God used a former enemy of the church, who was the author of much suffering by persecuted Christians, to be the main sufferer for Christ's sake.

Ananias followed the command of God. He went to the house of Judas and laid his hands on Paul. The laying on of hands was an act that served two purposes. First, it represented an act of prayer. Ananias was sent to pray that Paul's sight be restored and he receive the gift of the Holy Spirit. Second, it was a symbol of ordination or the transfer of authority. Ananias was sent to Paul in a similar manner in which God sent the prophet Samuel to anoint David the king of Israel (1 Samuel 16). When Ananias spoke and laid his hands on Paul, Paul miraculously received his sight. Ananias then led him to follow up the act of conversion with being baptized.

The Message of Paul's Conversion (9:20–22, 26–28)

After spending time with the disciples in Damascus, Paul began preaching the gospel. Verse 20 suggests that Paul began to preach immediately. There was no wasted time. Paul was clear about his calling.

Although Ananias's name is not specifically mentioned in these verses, we are to assume that his unique bond with Paul was what opened the doors for Paul to interact with other disciples at Damascus. Paul, now an apostle of Jesus Christ, was boldly proclaiming Jesus as the Christ, the Son of God. Now we find Paul, who was still being referred to as Saul, traveling to Jerusalem to join with the disciples there.

Again, because of Paul's past actions toward the church, he was not readily received (9:26). The Lord raised up another disciple in Barnabas to speak on behalf of Paul concerning the authenticity of his conversion and call to preach the gospel. Because of Barnabas's testimony concerning Paul, the apostles at Jerusalem were willing to accept him. Barnabas's word could be counted as trustworthy. He perhaps was one of the new converts as a result of Peter's preaching in Acts 2. He was one of the disciples noted by name for selling land and bringing the proceeds to the apostles to benefit those in need in the early church (4:36–37). His acts of kindness were so extraordinary that the apostles changed his name from Joseph to Barnabas, which means "son of encouragement" (4:36). If it were not for the courage of Ananias and the obedience of Barnabas, we would not have Paul the missionary.

Implications and Actions

Reaching the hard cases starts with our ability to articulate the events that led to a complete change or turn-around in our lives. Every relationship with Jesus Christ should begin with a time of enlightenment that is unforgettable and undeniable, whether the encounter took place in a worship service or a revival campaign or having lunch with a friend or simply riding along in the car alone. We must be willing and stand ready to use our personal experiences with Jesus as witnessing tools to reach others for Christ.

QUESTIONS

1. Reflecting on Paul's encounter with Jesus on the Damascus road, what elements of his experience are similar to your personal encounter with Jesus?

2. What qualities did Ananias and Barnabas display that made them successful in assisting Paul?

3. What meaning do you see in Paul's temporary blindness after his encounter with Jesus?

4. How can we use this passage to reach those whom we feel are unlikely to become a Christian?

NOTES

1. Unless otherwise indicated, all Scripture quotations in lessons 3–4, 6–8, 10–13 are taken from The Holy Bible, New International Version (North American Edition), copyright © 1973, 1978, 1984 by the International Bible Society.

FOCAL TEXT
Acts 11:1–26

BACKGROUND
Acts 10:1—11:26

MAIN IDEA
Led by God's Spirit, Peter and the church at Antioch crossed high cultural and theological barriers to reach people with the gospel.

QUESTION TO EXPLORE
How can you and your church cross over, break down, or go around barriers that keep you and your church from reaching people different from you with the good news about Jesus?

STUDY AIM
To identify barriers God is challenging me to cross in order to reach all people with the gospel

QUICK READ
Peter and the early church had to learn that they must cross all barriers that hindered sharing with everyone the gospel of salvation by God's grace solely through faith.

LESSON NINE
Cross Barriers to Reach Everyone

"This is America. We speak English." An irate caller said this in complaining to a Christian organization for the way the organization's phone had been answered. Because the organization's two major language groups speak English or Spanish, the answering system's preliminary greeting began, "Thank you for calling. For English, press *1*." Then, in Spanish, the caller was instructed to press *2* for Spanish. The angry caller complained (in English) to the representative who answered, "I shouldn't have to press *1* for English. This is America. We speak English." [1]

Hmm. But didn't Jesus say, "Go therefore and make disciples of all nations" (Matthew 28:19)? And didn't Jesus say, "You will be my witnesses in Jerusalem, in all Judea and Samaria, and to the ends of the earth" (Acts 1:8)?[2] Scripture shows that God has made his intent completely clear about whom he intends to love and reach, and God is going to cross barriers to seek to reach everyone. Moreover, God has also made clear that he expects all who belong to him to cross barriers to enjoy unhindered fellowship with one another.

Even though the Apostle Peter had heard Jesus himself issue the bold command in Matthew 28:19–20 and the bold statement in Acts 1:8, Peter was every bit as Jewish-centered as the caller was Anglo-centered. Acts 10:1—11:18 provides the account of how Peter had to learn that "God shows no partiality, but in every nation anyone who fears him and does what is right is acceptable to him" (Acts 10:34). The focal text, Acts 11:1–26, contains Peter's brief account of his experience in Acts 10 plus the experience of the Antioch church in reaching out to everyone.

In Acts 10:1—11:18, Peter and his fellow Jewish Christians actually had to confront two questions.[3] The first question had to do with salvation. Could Gentiles become Christians without fully becoming Jews, including keeping the Jewish rituals, certainly of circumcision? The second question had to do with fellowship. Could Jewish and Gentile Christians actually have full fellowship with one another, especially at the place where fellowship was most apparent—eating a meal together?

Answering these questions according to the gospel was hard. Actually, humanly speaking, doing so was impossible. At various points in Acts 10, we see that Peter was among the most reluctant of witnesses. Peter, who had walked and talked with Jesus, had to be dragged kicking and screaming to cross barriers to reach everyone, especially people who did not fit his ingrained cultural profile for potential disciples of Jesus. And would he eat a meal with those people? Absolutely not. But Peter changed. See how this happened and see how the church in Antioch reached out to everyone as you consider the Scriptures.

ACTS 11:1–26

[1] Now the apostles and the believers who were in Judea heard that the Gentiles had also accepted the word of God. [2] So when Peter went up to Jerusalem, the circumcised believers criticized him, [3] saying, "Why did you go to uncircumcised men and eat with them?" [4] Then Peter began to explain it to them, step by step, saying, [5] "I was in the city of Joppa praying, and in a trance I saw a vision. There was something like a large sheet coming down from heaven, being lowered by its four corners; and it came close to me. [6] As I looked at it closely I saw four-footed animals, beasts of prey, reptiles, and birds of the air. [7] I also heard a voice saying to me, 'Get up, Peter; kill and eat.' [8] But I replied, 'By no means, Lord; for nothing profane or unclean has ever entered my mouth.' [9] But a second time the voice answered from heaven, 'What God has made clean, you must not call profane.' [10] This happened three times; then everything was pulled up again to heaven. [11] At that very moment three men, sent to me from Caesarea, arrived at the house where we were. [12] The Spirit told me to go with them and not to make a distinction between them and us. These six brothers also accompanied me, and we entered the man's house. [13] He told us how he had seen the angel standing in his house and saying, 'Send to Joppa and bring Simon, who is called Peter; [14] he will give you a message by which you and your entire household will be saved.' [15] And as I began to speak, the Holy Spirit fell upon them just as it had upon us at the beginning. [16] And I remembered the word of the Lord, how he had said, 'John baptized with water, but you will be baptized with the Holy Spirit.' [17] If then God gave them the same gift that he gave us when we believed in the Lord Jesus Christ, who was I that I could hinder God?" [18] When they heard this, they were silenced. And they praised God, saying, "Then God has given even to the Gentiles the repentance that leads to life."

[19] Now those who were scattered because of the persecution that took place over Stephen traveled as far as Phoenicia, Cyprus, and Antioch, and they spoke the word to no one except Jews.

> [20] But among them were some men of Cyprus and Cyrene who, on coming to Antioch, spoke to the Hellenists also, proclaiming the Lord Jesus. [21] The hand of the Lord was with them, and a great number became believers and turned to the Lord. [22] News of this came to the ears of the church in Jerusalem, and they sent Barnabas to Antioch. [23] When he came and saw the grace of God, he rejoiced, and he exhorted them all to remain faithful to the Lord with steadfast devotion; [24] for he was a good man, full of the Holy Spirit and of faith. And a great many people were brought to the Lord. [25] Then Barnabas went to Tarsus to look for Saul, [26] and when he had found him, he brought him to Antioch. So it was that for an entire year they met with the church and taught a great many people, and it was in Antioch that the disciples were first called "Christians."

Two Big Questions (11:1–3)

You would have had to have been living in Judea in the first century A.D. to understand the shock in the statement in Acts 11:1. It's hard for us to imagine today that "the apostles and the believers who were in Judea" were concerned to hear "that the Gentiles had also accepted the word of God" (11:1). Cornelius had been attracted to worship and serve the God of Israel. But it was always understood that he and other such people weren't *really* Jews. They were *God-fearers*. They certainly weren't full-fledged Jews, because, for one reason or another, they hadn't undergone circumcision, the physical mark of being a Jew. They certainly weren't the kind of Jews you could sit down and enjoy a meal with. Could Gentiles really become faithful people of God without becoming Jews?

The background to the big shock in verse 1 is intensified by this question asked of Peter, "Why did you go to uncircumcised men and eat with them?" (11:2). Peter had gone to the home of Cornelius, who was not a Jew, and, what's more, *stayed there* "for several days" (11:48). Thus Peter obviously had eaten with Gentiles, and to do so was totally unacceptable according to the customs of first-century Judaism. Could Jews, even Jewish Christians, really engage in full fellowship with Gentiles as demonstrated by eating a meal together?

Before Peter's experience with Cornelius in Acts 10 he himself would have been asking the same question if a fellow Jewish Christian had done what he did. *Why did you eat with those Gentiles?* Peter himself believed that what he did in going to Cornelius's home was as wrong as wrong could be. There was no room in his theology for doing such a heinous act.

What Peter evidently had heard when Jesus uttered the words in Acts 1:8 was rather different from what Jesus meant. What Peter heard was likely this: *You will be my witnesses to the Jews in Jerusalem, the Jews in all Judea and Samaria, and the Jews to the ends of the earth.* If he had a liberal bent, he might have added, *and to the Gentiles if they are willing to become Jews first.*

Note that Peter's questioners began with their concern about with whom Peter had eaten and how he had broken the dietary laws rather than with the conversion of Cornelius and his friends. Their action thus underscored that they still were committed to the rituals of Judaism rather than to the grace of the Christian faith.

Peter's Experience (11:4–16)

Peter's questioners had in essence called him on the carpet. Peter, the reluctant witness, could point to a life-changing experience that had changed his mind and heart as much as his questioners needed their own minds and hearts changed.

Peter began to explain what had happened to him. The essence of this explanation is basically, *Look, this wasn't my idea. This was God's idea.* He went on, *I was in Joppa, minding my own business and praying to God. I had this "vision." In the vision I saw a large sheet being let down from heaven—from God. In it were all kinds of animals, and I mean ALL kinds of animals. Some of them were the kinds of animals on the forbidden list in the Book of Leviticus. As if that weren't bad enough, a voice—God's voice—told me to eat them. I refused, but God insisted. It seems now that I'd heard Jesus say something about that, but evidently I just didn't get it then (see Mark 7:15, 19). Anyway, God's voice came not once, not twice, but three times.*

While I was trying to figure out what to make of it, three men arrived from Caesarea (see Acts 10:17–29). I learned they had been sent by this

BIBLE STUDY RESOURCES IN OTHER LANGUAGES

BaptistWay Press, through financial resources provided by the Mary Hill Davis Offering for Texas Missions, provides Bible study materials in other languages for all age groups (see www.baptistwaypress.org). These materials are FREE to anyone, anywhere, who has access to the internet.

For adults, BaptistWay Press provides Bible study materials in these languages in addition to English: Cambodian, Chinese, Korean, Laotian, Spanish, Vietnamese, and Basic English. BaptistWay Press also provides early childhood, children, and youth Bible study materials in Spanish, including Vacation Bible School materials for early childhood and children. Use these materials yourself in your church's ministry, and please spread the word to others.

Gentile God-fearer, Cornelius. I found out later that he was "a centurion, an upright and God-fearing man, who is well spoken of by the whole Jewish nation" (10:22). Then, "the Spirit told me to go with them and not to make a distinction between them and us" (11:12). Now, I wasn't going by myself, for I knew there were going to be questions about this. So I took "six brothers" with me (11:12). When we got to the man's house, all of us went in. Then we found out that God had sent an angel to him to tell him to send for me! Cornelius explained that God had told him I was to give them a message that would result in his salvation and that of everybody who was part of his household. Are you starting to see why I went?

Peter continued to explain, leading his questioners to the climax. "The Holy Spirit fell upon them just as it had upon us at the beginning" (11:15; see 10:34–48). The experience of the Holy Spirit to which Peter was referring was the coming of the Spirit on the day of Pentecost in Acts 2. The coming of the Spirit verified the advance in the church's witness that took place at Cornelius's home even as the coming of the Spirit verified the advance in the church's witness that took place on the day of Pentecost.[4]

The attitude of Peter, the reluctant witness who was prejudiced against Gentiles, was changing. The reason it was changing—and had changed—had nothing to do with Peter and everything to do with God.

On his own, Peter would not have broken the Jewish customs and rituals by going to Cornelius's home. Too, on his own, Cornelius would have considered himself powerless to challenge them, even if he had wanted to do so. As Baptist New Testament scholar John Polhill comments on Peter's experience in the home of Cornelius, "Everyone there . . . was certain of one thing: *God* had brought them together."[5]

The Big Answer (11:17–18)

After Peter's recounting all of the ways in which God had led in Peter's experience with Cornelius, the conclusion was obvious. How could Peter—and by implication his questioners—try to withstand and "hinder God" (11:17)?

The Greek word translated "hinder" in Acts 11:17 is a key word in the Book of Acts. It's the same Greek word translated "prevent" in Acts 8:36 when the Ethiopian eunuch asked, "What is to prevent me from being baptized?" It's also used in Acts 10:47, where it is translated as "withhold" in the question, "Can anyone withhold the water for baptizing these people who have received the Holy Spirit just as we have?" The word will appear again in Acts 28:31, where Paul under house arrest in Rome is described as "proclaiming the kingdom of God and teaching about the Lord Jesus Christ with all boldness and without hindrance." The story of the Book of Acts is that the God's gospel simply will not be hindered. It will cross barriers to seek to reach everyone.

Peter's questioners got the message. So, "they praised God, saying, 'Then God has given even to the Gentiles the repentance that leads to

---

ANTIOCH

Antioch of Syria was a large cosmopolitan city of about 500,000 people. It was located about fifteen miles from the Mediterranean Sea. Ships were able to come up the Orontes River to Antioch's harbor. Various gods were worshiped in Antioch, and a Jewish community of about 25,000 to 50,000 in number was present.[10] Various peoples were present, too, including Greeks, Jews, Romans, and people "from Persia, India and even China."[11]

life'" (11:18). They understood at last that "by grace you have been saved through faith, and this is not your own doing; it is the gift of God—not the result of works, so that no one may boast" (Ephesians 2:8–9).

Unfortunately, the early Christians had to keep learning this lesson. They had to re-emphasize and re-learn it in Acts 15, and Paul's Letter to the Galatians contains another remedial lesson. Perhaps we wonder how they could not see that the gospel is for all people. They were bound by their culture in the same way that good Christians for hundreds of years could see no conflict between owning slaves, practicing racial discrimination, or looking down on people because they speak a different language or come from another culture. God often must be grieved that it takes us such a long time to unlearn wrong ideas and overcome old bad habits.

But it can be done. Fellow Baptist John Grisham's powerful novel, *A Time to Kill*, tells how an all-white jury in the South finally dealt with their prejudice in the trial of a black man.[6] It wasn't easy, though. It never is. Longtime faithful Christians can say things on the phone, in e-mails, or in person that show that in their heart of hearts they are failing to cross barriers to reach out with God's message of grace to everyone, certainly people different from them. Breakthroughs can occur, though, by the power of God.

Continuing to Cross Barriers (11:19–26)

Acts masterfully brings together in verse 19 two incidents that showed how the early church began aggressively and purposefully to cross barriers to reach everyone. First, Acts tells the story of the church at Antioch reaching out to everyone immediately after Peter's opponents acknowledged that "God has given even to the Gentiles the repentance that leads to life" (11:18). Second, Acts harks back to the story of Stephen in Acts 8:1. Stephen had proclaimed that the history of God's work with Israel had always involved Israel being on the move, following God where God led, beyond the geographical bounds of the land of Israel.

In the varied setting of cosmopolitan Antioch, the church took seriously Jesus' command to witness to everybody everywhere (Matt. 28:19–20; Acts 1:8). They proclaimed the gospel first to Jews but then

TABLE FELLOWSHIP

Is it true that we show we truly accept people to the degree that we're willing to sit down and have a meal with them? That was definitely the case with Jews, including Jewish Christians, in the time of the early church. The food laws in Leviticus spelled out what faithful Jews could and could not eat (see Leviticus 11:1–47; 20:24–26). In addition to the Jewish resistance in general to association with Gentiles, to eat a meal with a Gentile would have been unthinkable. Gentiles did not eat kosher food.

In Acts 11:2, Peter was asked why he dared to eat with non-Jews. Peter had to explain his dream, by which God instructed him, "What God has made clean, you must not call profane" (Acts 11:9). Earlier, Jesus himself had given instructions about clean and unclean (Mark 7:14–15, 18–23).

The concern about table fellowship continued to need solving in the early church. In Acts 15, the Jerusalem council (see lesson 11) developed a way to encourage table fellowship of both Jewish and Gentile Christians (see Acts 15:20, 29). Galatians 2:11–14 speaks of an occasion at Antioch in which Paul reprimanded Peter for not eating with Gentiles.

began to reach out beyond the bounds of Judaism to speak to "Hellenists" (11:20, NRSV) or "Greeks" (NASB, NIV)—"people who lived by Greek customs and culture."[7] The context indicates that these people most likely were non-Jews rather than simply Greek-speaking Jews.[8]

The church at Jerusalem wondered, *What's going on at Antioch?*[9] As had been so with the incident with Peter and Cornelius, the Jerusalem church found it necessary to investigate. They sent a person who recognized good things happening when he saw them. They sent Barnabas, who "was a good man, full of the Holy Spirit and of faith. And a great many people were brought to the Lord" (11:24).

Because the church at Antioch had caught so well Jesus' intent of crossing barriers to reach all people, we won't be surprised to see in Acts 13 that they continued to reach out to everyone everywhere, sending out the first missionary team (see lesson 10). How appropriate that the followers of Jesus were first called "Christians" at Antioch (11:26). As

DIFFERENT

Ron and Debbie's faith led them to become leaders in their community in making a difference for homeless people. The book *Same Kind of Different As Me* tells the true story of how a homeless man, Denver Moore, who had spent time in prison, and a wealthy international art dealer, Ron Hall, somehow became friends, and both had their lives changed through Christian ministry instigated by Ron's wife Debbie.

The book takes its title from a statement by the homeless man, who thought of himself as *different*. He came to realize that "everybody's different—the same kind of different as me."[12] Who are the *different* people in your community?

At least one of the many churches who regularly use BaptistWay Bible study materials has a significant ministry to the homeless of their community. Perhaps it's your church. Or perhaps your church should be doing this. Find the *different* people in your community to whom God is calling you to minister, and cross barriers to reach them.

Christians, we too are to be people who reach out to everyone everywhere for Jesus' sake.

Implications and Actions

Who are the left-out and looked-down-on people in your world? You know who they are. So does God, and God knows how you feel about them.

God has a dream ready for you. The dream will call for crossing barriers that keep you and your church from reaching out to everyone, even people who don't speak English or who aren't of your race, culture, or economic status.

QUESTIONS

1. Why do you think Jewish Christians had such difficulty in reaching out with the message of Jesus to people who were not Jews?

2. Why did Peter's dream picture animals?

3. What are some of the ways Peter realized God was at work in the experience with Cornelius?

4. What did the Holy Spirit's coming on Cornelius and his household signify?

5. Why did the church at Antioch grow?

6. If church members weren't already called Christians today, what would people call us?

7. What barriers do you, your Bible study group, or your church need to cross to reach people for Jesus?

NOTES

1. More than half of the people in the United States who speak a language other than English as their first language indicate that they speak English "very well." They deserve admiration for functioning in two languages, which most Anglos can't do. See http://usgovinfo.about.com/cs/censusstatistic/a/foreignlang.htm and http://www.census.gov/prod/2003pubs/c2kbr–29.pdf. Both accessed 2/9/12.

2. Unless otherwise indicated, all Scripture quotations in "Introducing the Book of Acts: Time to Act on Acts 1:8" and lessons 5 and 9 are taken from the New Revised Standard Version.

3. Frank Stagg, *The Book of Acts: The Early Struggle for an Unhindered Gospel* (Nashville, Tennessee: Broadman Press, 1955), 122.

4. John B. Polhill, *Acts,* The New American Commentary, vol. 26 (Nashville, Tennessee: Broadman Press, 1992), 264.

5. Polhill, 259, italics in original.

6. John Grisham, *A Time to Kill* (New York: Dell Books, paperback, 2009; Kindle edition, 2010).

7. Note on Acts 11:20 in NASB.

8. Polhill, 270, note 123.

9. Listen to Ken Medema's song, "What's Going On at Antioch?" in his CD *People of the Son.* See www.kenmedema.com. You can hear a sample of the song here: http://www.kenmedema.com/store/Scripts/prodView.asp?idproduct=77. Accessed 2/22/12.

10. Polhill, 268–269.

11. John R. W. Stott, *The Message of Acts,* The Bible Speaks Today (Downers Grove, Illinois: InterVarsity, 1994), 203.

12. Ron Hall and Denver Moore, *Same Kind of Different As Me: A Modern-Day Slave, an International Art Dealer, and the Unlikely Woman Who Bound Them Together* (Nashville, Tennessee: Thomas Nelson, 2006), Kindle location 2580–2581.

FOCAL TEXT
Acts 13:1–5, 13–14, 42–52

BACKGROUND
Acts 13

MAIN IDEA
The church at Antioch unhesitatingly obeyed the Spirit's leading to send missionaries out, and Barnabas and Paul boldly went, proclaiming Jesus to Jews and then to Gentiles.

QUESTIONS TO EXPLORE
How are we doing today in sending and being missionaries? Are you ready to go? to send?

STUDY AIM
To evaluate my participation in missions, whether sending or going

QUICK READ
Prior to Jesus' ascension, Jesus commissioned his followers to be witnesses to the farthest reaches of the world. Almost 2,000 years later, we remain engaged in this mission task.

LESSON TEN
Be Jesus' Witness Beyond Where You Are

"Do you think the church can send me? I really want to be sent by our church."

Ashley had no idea how much impact that simple question and comment would have on our church. She also didn't know another young woman had been in my office about six months earlier expressing her concerns about missions at our church. My conversation with Nicole was more pointed and animated.

"Does your church believe in missions?" Nicole asked me directly.

"Of course," I replied almost defensively.

"How many missionaries does your church support? Before I join, I need to know how personally invested your church is in the Great Commission."

I quickly defended the model of outsourcing missionaries to agencies and boards and tried to defend my position by expressing our long heritage in cooperative mission efforts.

"But, what about *this* church? How connected is *this* church to missions?" she asked.

So, unbeknownst to Ashley, my ecclesiology had collided with my missiology by the time she arrived in my office. After she expressed her desire to be sent by *her own* church, I looked directly at her and said confidently, "Absolutely. We will find a way to send you as a cross-cultural worker from this church."

Guess what? We did it! We now have a Direct Mission Sending Council and a committee that oversees mission strategy at our church. We have trained and commissioned fifteen cross-cultural workers from *our church* to serve in Asia, Africa, and Europe.

Acts 13 is just one of the biblical passages guiding our journey as a church in answering our personal call to the mission of God.[1]

ACTS 13:1–5, 13–14, 42–52

1 In the church at Antioch there were prophets and teachers: Barnabas, Simeon called Niger, Lucius of Cyrene, Manaen (who had been brought up with Herod the tetrarch) and Saul. 2 While they were worshiping the Lord and fasting, the Holy Spirit said, "Set apart for me Barnabas and Saul for the work to which I have called them." 3 So after they had fasted and prayed, they placed their hands on them and sent them off.

⁴ The two of them, sent on their way by the Holy Spirit, went down to Seleucia and sailed from there to Cyprus. ⁵ When they arrived at Salamis, they proclaimed the word of God in the Jewish synagogues. John was with them as their helper.

• • • • • • • • • • • • • • • • • • •

¹³ From Paphos, Paul and his companions sailed to Perga in Pamphylia, where John left them to return to Jerusalem. ¹⁴ From Perga they went on to Pisidian Antioch. On the Sabbath they entered the synagogue and sat down.

• • • • • • • • • • • • • • • • • • •

⁴² As Paul and Barnabas were leaving the synagogue, the people invited them to speak further about these things on the next Sabbath. ⁴³ When the congregation was dismissed, many of the Jews and devout converts to Judaism followed Paul and Barnabas, who talked with them and urged them to continue in the grace of God.

⁴⁴ On the next Sabbath almost the whole city gathered to hear the word of the Lord. ⁴⁵ When the Jews saw the crowds, they were filled with jealousy and talked abusively against what Paul was saying.

⁴⁶ Then Paul and Barnabas answered them boldly: "We had to speak the word of God to you first. Since you reject it and do not consider yourselves worthy of eternal life, we now turn to the Gentiles. ⁴⁷ For this is what the Lord has commanded us:

"'I have made you a light for the Gentiles,
    that you may bring salvation to the ends of the earth.'"

⁴⁸ When the Gentiles heard this, they were glad and honored the word of the Lord; and all who were appointed for eternal life believed.

⁴⁹ The word of the Lord spread through the whole region. ⁵⁰ But the Jews incited the God-fearing women of high standing and the leading men of the city. They stirred up persecution against Paul and Barnabas, and expelled them from their region. ⁵¹ So they shook the dust from their feet in protest against them and went to Iconium. ⁵² And the disciples were filled with joy and with the Holy Spirit.

God Always Has a Plan (13:1–5)

The cosmopolitan city of Antioch was the capital of the Roman province of Syria in the first century. It was a crossroads of the ancient world with a population that swelled at one point to almost 500,000 people. Heavily influenced by Greek culture, Antioch was nicknamed "The Beautiful" and famous for its long paved boulevard decorated with a colonnade of trees and fountains.

This ancient city was targeted by a group of unnamed evangelists fleeing persecution in Judea. On arriving in Antioch, these brave followers of The Way proclaimed the gospel to the cosmopolitan community with such fervor that a multi-cultural church was birthed (Acts 11:19–21). It grew into a remarkable congregation that eventually attracted the likes of Barnabas and Saul (Paul) to serve as leaders. And—the believers were first called "Christians" in Antioch (11:26). That would not be the only *first* for this church.

The opening verses of Acts 13 reveal a breadth of leadership in the church reflecting the diversity of the greater community itself. Two Africans (Simeon, Lucius, 13:1), a Levite (Barnabas), a rabbi (Saul), and one of royal heritage (Manaen) were at the helm of this strategic church.

In verse 2 we read that "they" were worshiping and fasting when God's Spirit prompted them to set apart Saul and Barnabas to fulfill their calling. "They" presumably refers to the entire church instead of just these leaders. Saul (by then known as Paul) would return to Antioch later and give a report to the entire church (14:26–28).

Upon the receipt of God's direction (Acts doesn't tell us *how* God spoke), the church responded in faith and obedience. They continued the spiritual practices of prayer and fasting as the process ensued. Finally, the very first missionaries in Christian history were commissioned and sent out.

Barnabas, a native of Cyprus, might have helped determine the initial target region of this first mission effort. The mission team (which now included John Mark) set sail from the Syrian mainland and arrived in Cyprus at the eastern seaboard city of Salamis. Barnabas and Saul were both trained in Jewish theology and steeped in Jewish culture. Therefore, the natural place to begin their work was among the Jewish population of this island.

So, what was God's plan? His plan was to mobilize a local church to become personally invested in his mission. The first-century world was a conglomeration of Greek, Roman, and Jewish influences. We should not be surprised a church comprised of various ethnicities and religious influences would be chosen by God to launch the great missionary enterprise designed to reach the cosmopolitan Roman Empire.

Commitment, Theology, and Common Sense (13:13–14, 42–45)

Without question, answering the call of God required commitment and dedication. Paul (referred to as "Paul" in Acts 13:9 and never again in the New Testament called "Saul") gave the rest of his life to this endeavor. He endured persecution, fatigue, misunderstandings, beatings, and abandonment.[2] According to Christian tradition, he finally died as a martyr at the hands of the Roman Emperor, Nero.

In order to take the message of Christ to the people of Asia Minor, Macedonia, and beyond, Paul had to withstand the rigors of travel in the ancient world. For example, after sailing to Perga (Acts 13:13), they trekked 100 miles by foot to the highland city of Pisidian Antioch (elevation 3,600 feet). When was the last time you or I *walked* 100 miles? Was it too rigorous for John Mark? Was he upset that Paul seemed to be the leader of the team instead of Barnabas? Was he in conflict with Paul theologically? We don't know. Luke doesn't tell us why John Mark left the mission, but he offered a hint at his feelings toward the young helper in his comments later in Acts 15:38 with the accusation that John Mark "deserted" the team.

The point is this: *Taking the gospel to the world required a serious commitment in the first century.* Crossing cultural, geographical, and religious boundaries was fraught with challenges and complexities. Paul persevered and answered the call. How about us? How are we handling the various obstacles in our path as we seek to take the gospel to the ends of the earth? In the twenty-first century, commitment is still vital to the mission task.

Notice also Paul was driven by a core theological commitment as stated in Romans 1:16. The gospel was for the Jew first and then the Gentile. In fact, he went so far as to say he would be willing to be "cursed and cut off" from Christ if that would guarantee his Jewish brothers and sisters would accept Jesus as Messiah (Romans 9:1–5). Paul's theology shaped his missiology. It was common practice for him to search for a

OUR CHURCH AND MISSIONS

More than two years ago, our church joined another Texas Baptist church in a joint partnership in training and sending a young couple to live as cross-cultural workers in West Africa. Our churches combined our respective giftedness and crafted an alliance that has resulted in this couple serving their first two-year term working among a remote, unreached people group.

Ben and Melissa are currently living in West Africa and are overseeing our work in two different regions of a West African nation. Their home church nurtured them as children and blessed them in their journey to seminary. Our church became their church home during seminary. They began to sense the call of God to *go*. They wanted their churches to send them.

Our church has participated in the development of a year-long curriculum that trains people to live in a cross-cultural environment as witnesses for Jesus. The couple completed their training and submitted themselves to the sending process as outlined by our two churches *together*. Both of our churches commissioned them in two separate worship services. Both of our churches provide the financial support for their work. Their home church pastor and I visit them in West Africa and participate in the oversight of their strategy and work.

We have agreed to work with indigenous partners as a key part of our strategy. Ben and Melissa have built a team comprised of these local believers, and God has blessed this work tremendously! We are in the midst of the most significant spiritual awakening we have ever known among this particular people group. Two Baptist churches are collaborating together in going and sending. We are seeking to be Jesus' witnesses beyond where we are.

synagogue in every town he visited (Acts 13:5, 14; 14:1). His message to the Jews was rooted solidly in the Hebrew Scriptures. He pointed his own people to the prophets and to the promises of God. He boldly proclaimed Jesus as the fulfillment of prophecy and the heir to the throne of David. His compelling message culminated with the reality of the resurrection of Jesus Christ from the dead.

Throughout his missionary work, Paul had a measure of success in proclaiming the gospel of Jesus Christ to his fellow Jews. Many Jewish people embraced these claims and became servants of the Messiah. However, in the early days of Paul's ministry, it became apparent his primary target for evangelism was the Gentile population of the first century.

Paul's missiological strategy was not just theologically informed, but it also contained an element of common sense. What do I mean by that? The synagogues of the first-century world included faithful Jews and Gentiles known as *God-fearers* (see lesson 9). They worshiped the God of Israel even though they were not considered full-fledged Jews. These Gentiles served as the bridge to the rest of the Gentile community. Paul's experience in Pisidian Antioch is just one example of this (13:14–48, especially 13:16, 26, 43, 48).

After Paul preached a sermon in the synagogue based on the Hebrew Scriptures and the life of Jesus, the people responded favorably (13:42). Paul and Barnabas were invited back to speak the very next Sabbath. Word spread from the converts to Judaism to the broader Gentile community during the intervening week. The next Sabbath was a sell-out! Gentiles came en masse to the meeting (13:44). Instead of rejoicing at a full house for worship, though, the Jewish leaders were angry and jealous (13:45).

However, the die was cast. Paul witnessed a dramatic response from a Gentile audience, and his ministry was catapulted beyond the synagogue into the marketplace.

Crossing Barriers with the Gospel Message (13:46–52)

Paul recognized the hand of God in the meeting in Pisidian Antioch. He had spent enough time in Syrian Antioch to see God working beyond Judaism. He immediately seized this moment theologically and pragmatically when he proclaimed his pivotal turn to the Gentiles (13:46). The new wine of the gospel could not be contained in old wine skins. Gentiles populated the earth, and the witness to Jesus was to be proclaimed to the ends of the earth (1:8). Paul set the stage for the rest of his missionary career as he quoted and applied Isaiah 49:6 to his day (Acts 13:47).

What was the Gentile audience's response? Luke said, "They were glad and honored the word of the Lord" (13:48). He closed this remark with a phrase that has puzzled interpreters for centuries: "and all who were appointed for eternal life believed." Wow. That closing would swell the chest of any Calvinist worth his or her salt! But, what does it mean?

This controversial statement is juxtaposed to the seemingly willful rejection of the gospel by many Jews (13:45–46). It also must be read in light of Paul's use of Joel's prophecy in Romans 10:13, "Everyone who calls on the name of the Lord will be saved" (see Joel 2:32).

Doubtless, the phrasing of Acts 13:48 is pointed and clear. However, I would temper Calvinistic excitement about the verse with the simple truth that both God's power and human decision are involved in salvation. No one can be saved without God's power. In this very passage, some chose to reject, and others chose to obey. The mystery of salvation will never be fully embraced if we choose to exclude either God or human beings in the process. People are not saved on their own merit, independently of the work of God. Yet, God works within the dynamics of human personalities. I will choose to praise God for God's grace and to walk carefully in any interpretation of this passage that lacks the humility afforded such a divine mystery as the salvation of a human soul.

One thing is certain, the gospel is the power of God (Romans 1:16; Acts 13:49). God honors its proclamation. As this chapter concludes (Acts 13), the movement of God was in full swing, and the disciples were living in the joy of obedience and usefulness.

Our Response

Most of us believe God's mission is important and should be a priority. However, we often believe it is not *our* responsibility to make sure it is accomplished. After all, we are just common people. We get up in the morning, get the kids off to school, drop off the dry cleaning, and go to work. We pick up the kids from their various activities, go home, cook supper, watch a little television, help with homework, and go to bed. Sure, someone needs to be paying attention to God's mission—but surely not us! We are just normal people.

The mission of God is for *professionals*—right? Those *missionaries* can cross cultures in a single bound. They can learn multiple languages at ease. They are the ones who shoulder the responsibility for God's mission.

Actually, the responsibility for God's mission belongs to *all of us.* We are either going or sending. But those are our only two options. Either we are called to go, or we are responsible to assist others in going. That's it. Not everyone from Antioch went on the team. However, the entire church was part of the process.

God has called you to participate in his mission. Are you called to go? *Go!* If not, you *are* called to send. How are you personally involved in sending those who are called to go?

QUESTIONS

1. After studying Acts 11 (lesson nine) and Acts 13, what are your impressions of the church in Antioch?

2. What challenges did the first missionary team sent out from a local church face?

3. How would you describe your personal responsibility in the mission of God?

4. What are some concrete examples of your church's personal investment in the mission of God?

NOTES

1. Unless otherwise indicated, all Scripture quotations in lessons 3–4, 6–8, 10–13 are taken from The Holy Bible, New International Version (North American Edition), copyright © 1973, 1978, 1984 by the International Bible Society.

2. See 2 Corinthians 12:23–29.

MAIN IDEA

The church decided that they must focus on Jesus and his grace rather than on non-essential human requirements about salvation and relating to people.

QUESTION TO EXPLORE

What non-essential matters do we allow, whether by custom or conviction, to get in the way of focusing on Jesus and his grace?

STUDY AIM

To focus on Jesus and his grace rather than on non-essential human requirements about salvation and relating to people

QUICK READ

At the Jerusalem conference, the first-century church affirmed that salvation comes through faith in Jesus Christ alone, with nothing else required.

LESSON ELEVEN
Keep Focused On What's Essential

When we started our contemporary service at a church I served, we hoped that the more informal service in a more casual setting would attract some people to our church who might feel uncomfortable in our more traditional service. Several weeks after we had started the new service, I was standing in the vestibule of the church before the service when I spotted a young couple with two small children standing just inside the door. The young couple had coffee cups in hand. I observed immediately from their dress and from the tattoos and the piercings that they were not typical First Baptist people. I was elated. I introduced myself to them and walked with them into the sanctuary and helped them find a place.

I immediately turned my attention to other people. When the service started, I stood up to welcome everyone, and I noticed that this family was no longer in the sanctuary. After the service, I discovered the reason for their absence. One of our members apparently informed them they were not allowed to bring food or drink into the sanctuary, and so they just got up and left the service.

Which is more important, to protect our property or to provide a welcoming environment for people to participate in worship? Which is really central, and which is non-essential?

That is not a new issue. The first-century Christians faced that issue in one of the most important moments in the early church, an event we sometimes refer to as the first church business meeting.[1]

ACTS 15:1-29

[1] Some men came down from Judea to Antioch and were teaching the brothers: "Unless you are circumcised, according to the custom taught by Moses, you cannot be saved." [2] This brought Paul and Barnabas into sharp dispute and debate with them. So Paul and Barnabas were appointed, along with some other believers, to go up to Jerusalem to see the apostles and elders about this question. [3] The church sent them on their way, and as they traveled through Phoenicia and Samaria, they told how the Gentiles had been converted. This news made all the brothers very glad. [4] When they came to Jerusalem, they were welcomed

by the church and the apostles and elders, to whom they reported everything God had done through them.

⁵ Then some of the believers who belonged to the party of the Pharisees stood up and said, "The Gentiles must be circumcised and required to obey the law of Moses."

⁶ The apostles and elders met to consider this question. ⁷ After much discussion, Peter got up and addressed them: "Brothers, you know that some time ago God made a choice among you that the Gentiles might hear from my lips the message of the gospel and believe. ⁸ God, who knows the heart, showed that he accepted them by giving the Holy Spirit to them, just as he did to us. ⁹ He made no distinction between us and them, for he purified their hearts by faith. ¹⁰ Now then, why do you try to test God by putting on the necks of the disciples a yoke that neither we nor our fathers have been able to bear? ¹¹ No! We believe it is through the grace of our Lord Jesus that we are saved, just as they are."

¹² The whole assembly became silent as they listened to Barnabas and Paul telling about the miraculous signs and wonders God had done among the Gentiles through them. ¹³ When they finished, James spoke up: "Brothers, listen to me. ¹⁴ Simon has described to us how God at first showed his concern by taking from the Gentiles a people for himself. ¹⁵ The words of the prophets are in agreement with this, as it is written:

¹⁶ "'After this I will return
       and rebuild David's fallen tent.
    Its ruins I will rebuild,
       and I will restore it,
¹⁷ that the remnant of men may seek the Lord,
       and all the Gentiles who bear my name,
       says the Lord, who does these things'
¹⁸ that have been known for ages.

¹⁹ "It is my judgment, therefore, that we should not make it difficult for the Gentiles who are turning to God. ²⁰ Instead we should write to them, telling them to abstain from food polluted by idols, from sexual immorality, from the meat of strangled animals and from blood. ²¹ For Moses has been preached in every

city from the earliest times and is read in the synagogues on every Sabbath."

[22] Then the apostles and elders, with the whole church, decided to choose some of their own men and send them to Antioch with Paul and Barnabas. They chose Judas (called Barsabbas) and Silas, two men who were leaders among the brothers. [23] With them they sent the following letter:

> The apostles and elders, your brothers,
>
> To the Gentile believers in Antioch, Syria and Cilicia:
>
> Greetings.

[24] We have heard that some went out from us without our authorization and disturbed you, troubling your minds by what they said. [25] So we all agreed to choose some men and send them to you with our dear friends Barnabas and Paul— [26] men who have risked their lives for the name of our Lord Jesus Christ. [27] Therefore we are sending Judas and Silas to confirm by word of mouth what we are writing. [28] It seemed good to the Holy Spirit and to us not to burden you with anything beyond the following requirements: [29] You are to abstain from food sacrificed to idols, from blood, from the meat of strangled animals and from sexual immorality. You will do well to avoid these things.

> Farewell.

The Conflict (15:1–5)

Cradled in Jerusalem, the first church consisted only of Jews who had become Christians and continued to follow Jewish customs. However, when the church expanded beyond the borders of Jerusalem and beyond the ranks of the Jews, Jewish customs came into conflict with the cultural practices of the new Gentile Christians, threatening division in the church.

On one side were those convinced that Christians must continue to follow the Jewish customs. Luke identified those holding this view as "believers who belonged to the party of the Pharisees" (Acts 15:5). Who were they? Some commentators identify them with the delegation sent to Antioch by James cited in Galatians 2:12. They believed that faith in Jesus Christ is not sufficient to bring a person to salvation. A person must also observe the Jewish religious rituals and follow the Jewish law. These requirements strike at the heart of the gospel that offers salvation to "everyone who believes" in Jesus (John 3:16). Nevertheless, in the early church one group of Christians attached these Jewish requirements to faith as a prerequisite to salvation (Acts 15:5).

On the other side of the issue were those whose experience prompted them to welcome into the church any person of any ethnic or religious group who simply acknowledged Jesus as Lord (15:2-4). This view permeated the newly-formed church at Antioch. Because of their experience, Paul and Barnabas also lined up on this side. In order to defend this position, the church at Antioch commissioned Paul and Barnabas to go to Jerusalem to defend the gospel.

On their way to Jerusalem, they addressed the issue with the various groups they encountered. However, note that they did not argue from Old Testament precedent. They simply shared what they experienced on their missionary journey through Asia Minor. When Paul and Barnabas preached the gospel, Gentiles responded in faith and gave evidence of conversion, just as the Jews who responded had done. Why then should the church add to what God had already done? The conference in Jerusalem provided each side the opportunity to explain their position.

The Conversation (15:6–12)

A large number of Christian leaders gathered in Jerusalem for the conference, including both "the apostles" (probably using this term in its more general reference to those set aside for the gospel, not just the original Twelve) and "elders" (15:6). Acts specifically identifies only Peter, Paul, Barnabas, and James, the brother of Jesus, who presided over the conference. Even though many leaders participated in the discussion ("After much discussion," 15:7), Acts does not include their comments. Acts presents only a summary of Peter's presentation (15:7–11) and a brief synopsis of the presentation by Paul and Barnabas (15:12).

Peter did not argue about the issue. Instead, he told the story of his experience in Caesarea when he shared the gospel with Cornelius and his family (15:7–11; see 10:1—11:18). Peter acknowledged that God's hand guided his experience with Cornelius. To therefore claim that the conversion of Cornelius and his family was not genuine questioned the character of God.

On an earlier trip to Jerusalem Peter presented the same story about his experience with Cornelius, confessing that he himself was startled by what happened at Cornelius's house. Yet, he could not question what God clearly confirmed. Peter concluded, "Who was I to think that I could oppose God?" (11:17). Peter presented essentially the same story and raised the same question in his speech at the Jerusalem council described in Acts 15.

Paul and Barnabas then shared their experiences, apparently evoking a reverent awe from those who listened (15:12). Like Peter, they did not argue the issue. They simply related stories of their experiences throughout Asia Minor where individuals with no Jewish background experienced salvation through their faith in Jesus Christ without submitting to or following any of the customs of Jewish law (15:12). Paul and Barnabas, as with Peter, acknowledged that these stories were not about what they had done but about what God had done. And they might well have repeated Peter's earlier question: "Who was I to think that I could oppose God?" (11:17).

The Conclusion (15:13–21)

Since there were two sides in the conflict, Luke's failure to include the testimony by those who opposed the position verbalized by Peter and Paul and Barnabas may perplex us. This could be an example of the old dictum: *Winners write the history.* Since the church embraced the viewpoint espoused by Peter, Paul, and Barnabas, perhaps Luke chose to ignore the arguments on the other side of the issue. Or maybe those holding the opposing position simply melted before the force of the testimony presented. In either case, the church clearly reached a conclusion, and James, as the spokesman for the church in Jerusalem, articulated that conclusion.

Notice that those who attended the conference did not seem to vote on one or the other position. After the time of discussion, James simply summarized the decision that the assembly clearly embraced. To the

THE CHURCH AT ANTIOCH

Next to the church at Jerusalem, no church played a more important role in the spread of Christianity than the church in Antioch of Syria. Nicolas, one of the first deacons, was from the city of Antioch (Acts 6:5). We do not know whether he played any part in establishing the church at Antioch. Acts 11:19 indicates that the church in Antioch was established by some of the Christians scattered by the persecution that followed Stephen's death.

So many responded to the gospel in Antioch that the Christians in Jerusalem sent Barnabas to investigate. He affirmed the new Christians in Antioch and encouraged them to remain faithful to their new faith (11:22–23). Later, the church at Antioch would commission Barnabas and Saul to go on the first mission trip (13:1–3). Antioch, and not Jerusalem, became the launching pad for the spread of the gospel.

overwhelming majority of the assembly, this new paradigm for salvation in God's kingdom was a directive from God.

Following the common pattern by New Testament Christians, James saw this new development to be a fulfillment of Scripture. Drawing together quotes of "the words from the prophets," James concluded that what happened was nothing less than a fulfillment of what the prophets had foretold centuries earlier (15:16–18; see Amos 9:11–12; Jeremiah 12:15; Isaiah 45:21). James drew the heart of his scriptural summary from Amos 9:12, where the prophet pointed to a time when "all the nations that bear my name" will be included among his remnant.

At this point, we become aware of a second issue confronting the first-century Christians gathered in Jerusalem. The first issue concerned the nature of salvation, and the Christians at the conference concluded that salvation through Christ is available to everyone who believes (Acts 15:19). In addition to this theological dimension, the conflict between Gentile Christians and Jewish Christians also had a sociological dimension concerning the nature of fellowship between those who believe. On this issue the solution was not as simple.

Even though Gentiles and Jews could experience salvation in the same way, cultural differences created tension when Gentile and Jewish Christians related to one another in the fellowship of the church. The

---

CASE STUDY

Put yourself in the situation described at the beginning of the lesson. The new couple, with coffee cups and donuts in their hands, has entered the sanctuary with their two children. You know they are guests who have never attended the church before. You watch them walk past the sign on the door to the sanctuary that says, "No Food or Drinks Inside," which they either do not see or choose to ignore. How will you respond?

Christians gathered at Jerusalem apparently discussed this issue as well although Acts reveals nothing about the nature of this discussion. Instead, James simply announced the conclusion, articulating it in his closing remarks. To facilitate fellowship between Jewish Christians and Gentile Christians, James suggested four basic guidelines (see 15:20–21). Three of these guidelines had to do with etiquette for table fellowship ("abstain from food polluted by idols," "abstain from . . . the meat of strangled animals and from blood"). One of them related to moral character ("abstain . . . from sexual immorality"). We must remember, however, that these guidelines had nothing to do with salvation. They were guidelines to facilitate fellowship between those who were already saved.

The Communication (15:22–29)

Once God clearly revealed his will to those who attended the conference in Jerusalem, these leaders communicated that decision to the churches in Antioch, Syria, and Cilicia by sending a letter (15:23). They authorized Judas and Silas to accompany Barnabas and Paul as they delivered the letter to these churches. We don't have any further reference to Judas. However, Silas became Paul's companion. He was obviously from the Jerusalem church (15:22). Yet, he bought into Paul's vision of the church and became his co-worker in the greater Gentile ministry.

The letter disavowed the earlier unauthorized group from Jerusalem who "disturbed" the Christians in Antioch (15:24). The letter then clarified the decision reached by the Jerusalem Council (15:28–29). On the matter of salvation, faith alone is required. On the matter of fellowship, the letter presented to the Gentiles the same guidelines cited in Acts 15:22, not as laws to which they must submit in order to be saved but as proscriptions they should follow to enhance the relationships between Gentile and Jewish Christians. So the first Christians avoided adding extraneous elements to the faith that would distract them from the central truth of the gospel—that salvation is available to all people through simple faith in Jesus Christ.

Implications and Actions

Consider two specific points at which we can learn from these first Christians. To begin with, the Christians at Antioch who sent the delegation to Jerusalem provide insight into how to handle conflict today. On the one hand, they were unwilling to ignore the tension between them and their fellow Christians in Jerusalem as if no problem existed. On the other hand, they were not willing to yield to the pressures exerted by some in the Jerusalem church to affirm a position they did not believe. Instead, they acknowledged the problem and then attempted to dissolve the problem if possible, not by arguments but by telling the stories of what God had done in their lives and in the lives of others.

In addition, the Christians at the Jerusalem conference remained focused on the central issue of salvation and refused to be sidetracked by the non-essential human requirements the Judaizers wanted to impose. They recognized the difference between the essential and the non-essential. May we follow their pattern today.

QUESTIONS

1. What divisive issues exist in your church that no one is willing to address?

2. How does the pattern of decision-making in your church compare to the pattern reflected in our text?

3. Do you think people want to add to the requirements to salvation even today?

4. What are some of the elements they want to add?

5. What can you do to affirm the decision reached by the Jerusalem Conference concerning the requirement for salvation?

NOTES ————————————————————————————

1. Unless otherwise indicated, all Scripture quotations in lessons 3–4, 6–8, 10–13 are taken from The Holy Bible, New International Version (North American Edition), copyright © 1973, 1978, 1984 by the International Bible Society.

FOCAL TEXT
Acts 16:25–34; 17:1–4, 16–34

BACKGROUND
Acts 15:36—17:34

MAIN IDEA
Paul communicated the gospel in diverse ways to diverse people, relating to them in ways appropriate to their needs and background.

QUESTION TO EXPLORE
How can we communicate the gospel to diverse people?

STUDY AIM
To commit myself to learning to share the gospel with diverse people

QUICK READ
Wherever Paul's travels took him, his message was always the same—Jesus is the Christ. However, his methods were diverse, taking into account the needs and the background of the people.

LESSON TWELVE
Witness in Diverse Ways to Diverse People

A popular evangelist was leading an evangelistic meeting in a local church. After one sermon a woman walked up to him and said, "I don't like the way you share the gospel."

The evangelist looked at her and said, "I don't like the way you *don't* share the gospel."

There is no one way to witness to others about God's love in Jesus Christ. The message of God's grace through Jesus' death on the cross for the forgiveness of people's sins is the same for everyone. How that message is communicated can be as diverse as the people one encounters, though. The message does not change, but the methods can change.[1]

ACTS 16:25–34

25 About midnight Paul and Silas were praying and singing hymns to God, and the other prisoners were listening to them. 26 Suddenly there was such a violent earthquake that the foundations of the prison were shaken. At once all the prison doors flew open, and everybody's chains came loose. 27 The jailer woke up, and when he saw the prison doors open, he drew his sword and was about to kill himself because he thought the prisoners had escaped. 28 But Paul shouted, "Don't harm yourself! We are all here!"

29 The jailer called for lights, rushed in and fell trembling before Paul and Silas. 30 He then brought them out and asked, "Sirs, what must I do to be saved?"

31 They replied, "Believe in the Lord Jesus, and you will be saved—you and your household." 32 Then they spoke the word of the Lord to him and to all the others in his house. 33 At that hour of the night the jailer took them and washed their wounds; then immediately he and all his family were baptized. 34 The jailer brought them into his house and set a meal before them; he was filled with joy because he had come to believe in God—he and his whole family.

ACTS 17:1–4, 16–34

1 When they had passed through Amphipolis and Apollonia, they came to Thessalonica, where there was a Jewish synagogue.

² As his custom was, Paul went into the synagogue, and on three Sabbath days he reasoned with them from the Scriptures, ³ explaining and proving that the Christ had to suffer and rise from the dead. "This Jesus I am proclaiming to you is the Christ," he said. ⁴ Some of the Jews were persuaded and joined Paul and Silas, as did a large number of God-fearing Greeks and not a few prominent women.

•   •   •   •   •   •   •   •   •   •   •   •   •   •   •   •   •   •   •

¹⁶ While Paul was waiting for them in Athens, he was greatly distressed to see that the city was full of idols. ¹⁷ So he reasoned in the synagogue with the Jews and the God-fearing Greeks, as well as in the marketplace day by day with those who happened to be there. ¹⁸ A group of Epicurean and Stoic philosophers began to dispute with him. Some of them asked, "What is this babbler trying to say?" Others remarked, "He seems to be advocating foreign gods." They said this because Paul was preaching the good news about Jesus and the resurrection. ¹⁹ Then they took him and brought him to a meeting of the Areopagus, where they said to him, "May we know what this new teaching is that you are presenting? ²⁰ You are bringing some strange ideas to our ears, and we want to know what they mean." ²¹ (All the Athenians and the foreigners who lived there spent their time doing nothing but talking about and listening to the latest ideas.)

²² Paul then stood up in the meeting of the Areopagus and said: "Men of Athens! I see that in every way you are very religious. ²³ For as I walked around and looked carefully at your objects of worship, I even found an altar with this inscription: TO AN UNKNOWN GOD. Now what you worship as something unknown I am going to proclaim to you.

²⁴ "The God who made the world and everything in it is the Lord of heaven and earth and does not live in temples built by hands. ²⁵ And he is not served by human hands, as if he needed anything, because he himself gives all men life and breath and everything else. ²⁶ From one man he made every nation of men, that they should inhabit the whole earth; and he determined the times set for them and the exact places where they should live. ²⁷ God did

this so that men would seek him and perhaps reach out for him and find him, though he is not far from each one of us. [28] 'For in him we live and move and have our being.' As some of your own poets have said, 'We are his offspring.'

[29] "Therefore since we are God's offspring, we should not think that the divine being is like gold or silver or stone—an image made by man's design and skill. [30] In the past God overlooked such ignorance, but now he commands all people everywhere to repent. [31] For he has set a day when he will judge the world with justice by the man he has appointed. He has given proof of this to all men by raising him from the dead."

[32] When they heard about the resurrection of the dead, some of them sneered, but others said, "We want to hear you again on this subject." [33] At that, Paul left the Council. [34] A few men became followers of Paul and believed. Among them was Dionysius, a member of the Areopagus, also a woman named Damaris, and a number of others.

The Content of the Message

Luke records the beginning of Paul's second missionary journey in Acts 15:36. Between Acts 15:36 and Acts 16:24, we find Paul and Barnabas going separate ways with the intent of visiting the churches already established. However, the Holy Spirit had a different plan for Paul, Silas, and Timothy. One night Paul received a vision of a man calling him to come over into Macedonia. Paul followed that call, taking the gospel into what we often consider the Western world for the first time. Paul and his companions met a prominent woman named Lydia in Philippi in Macedonia. She was already a worshiper of God. Paul shared the gospel with her, and she became a believer in the Lord Jesus Christ. Later Paul and Silas would be thrown into prison for casting the demon of fortune-telling out of a young girl.

From the time Paul and Silas were thrown into jail in Acts 16:23 until Paul's encounter with the philosophers on the Areopagus (Mars Hill) in Acts 17:18, we see how the gospel was shared faithfully to diverse people in diverse situations.

The jailor in Philippi asked Paul and Silas in 16:30, "Sirs, what must I do to be saved?" Paul and Silas both answered, "Believe in the Lord Jesus, and you will be saved—you and your household" (Acts 16:31). Paul and Silas never compromised the gospel. The gospel seems very simple, but it is the power of God to everyone who believes (Romans 1:16). The gospel is simple from the human point of view but not from God's point of view. Jesus died to forgive people of their sins and was raised from the dead by the power of God to provide salvation.

We see in Acts 17:1–4 how Paul relied on the Scriptures to explain to the synagogue in Thessalonica that Jesus was the Christ (*Anointed One* or *Messiah*) promised in the Scriptures. The Scriptures Paul was reasoning from were what we know as the Old Testament, the Bible of Paul's day.

Similarly, in 17:10–12, Paul stayed faithful to the gospel as he proclaimed Jesus to the synagogue in Berea. The Bereans were open to the gospel because of their love for examining the Old Testament Scriptures to see where God was leading.

Sometimes Christians become overwhelmed by the many spiritual messages in our world today. Those who question all knowledge, institutions, and authority figures, including Scripture and the church, while at the same time showing some interest in things of the spirit (small *s*) can intimidate a Christian into not sharing the gospel. But we must

AREOPAGUS

The Areopagus is a big piece of rock (*pagos*) northwest of the Acropolis in Athens, Greece. The word *Aeropagus* is a compound word from ancient Greek—*areios* and *pagos*. Ares was the Greek god of war, and *pagos* means rock. So the *Areopagus* is *Ares Rock* or *Rock of Ares*.

Sometimes the hill is known as Mars Hill since Mars was the Roman god of war. The Areopagus functioned as the high court of appeal for criminal and civil cases. The name was used both of the prominent rock and of the group who met there. It was on this hill and to this group that Paul delivered his famous sermon "TO AN UNKNOWN GOD" (Acts 17:23). Paul stood on the hill where the court of appeals met to make his appeal for God's revelation of himself in Jesus Christ.

remember that the gospel is the power of God to salvation. We are not convincing or persuading someone to believe. We are simply sharing God's plan in Jesus; the Holy Spirit will do the convincing.

The Context of the Method

When Paul and his companions set out on this second missionary journey, they soon found it would take them into different countries with diverse nationalities. They would go through Asia Minor and into Macedonia and Greece. They would encounter Greeks and Romans, and Gentiles as well as Jews. In these encounters, we see how Paul and his companions communicated the gospel in diverse ways.

For instance, the jailor in Philippi would be considered a *raw pagan*. How does one share the gospel with someone who has no clue about Jesus or salvation? No doubt the jailor had been listening to Paul and

CASE STUDY

Paul and his family lived in an upscale neighborhood in a suburb of Houston, Texas. Since Houston is such a diverse city with many nationalities and many religions, it was not unusual that Paul's neighbors were from India and were Hindu. In fact, Paul and his family had been transferred to Houston from Bangalore, India, by a major corporation.

Paul and his family became friends with their new neighbors and socialized together on several occasions. Since Paul was a member of a local Baptist church he thought he would invite his neighbors to attend his church with him. The neighbors accepted Paul's invitation to attend a service.

Later Paul visited with the father of the family and talked with him about Jesus. The man said that he had no trouble accepting Jesus as *a god*. Paul became excited about this statement, thinking that the man was accepting Jesus as Savior. If Paul had been more familiar with Hinduism, what would have raised red flags about his accepting Jesus as *a god*? (Hinduism accepts the existence of multiple gods.) How would you have addressed the neighbor's response?

Silas as they were praying and singing hymns to God. His question to Paul and Silas was what to do to be "saved" (Acts 16:30). Paul and Silas took him where he was and gave a simple witness, "Believe in the Lord Jesus, and you will be saved" (16:31). The context of the question was salvation, and the content of the message was salvation. *As we witness, we need to listen to what a person says to tell where that person is in his or her search for Jesus.*

When Paul and Silas came to Thessalonica, they went into a Jewish synagogue (17:1–4), as they customarily did. Since the Jews would be familiar with the Scriptures (Old Testament), Paul used these Scriptures to witness to Jesus as the Christ. The Christ (*Messiah*) was a prophetic hope for all Jews. This idea would be familiar to them. This same method was used by Paul with the Bereans (17:10–12). *When we witness to people, we need to begin with something that is familiar to them. By doing this we can gain an opportunity to share the gospel.*

Paul's encounter with Greek philosophers in Acts 17:16–34 challenged him to address their interest in the many gods. He knew that they were a religious people because of the number of idols and objects of worship in their city. This encounter took place on what was called the *Areopagus* (see small article, "Areopagus"). The Romans called this same prominent hill *Mars Hill* after the Roman god of war, Mars. The word *Areopagus* noted not only this prominent rocky hill, but it also defined the group that met there. Those who comprised the Areopagus were noted city leaders, philosophers, and legal experts. People who were guilty of crimes were sometimes brought here to be tried. So Paul found himself on this prominent hill being engaged by these bright and talented minds. The Epicureans believed that there were gods but the gods were remote and did not care for humankind. They believed that pleasure was the chief end to be sought. The Stoics on the other hand believed that everything was god. They believed in fate, that whatever happened was god's will.

Paul addressed two areas of interest to these philosophers. First, he addressed their interest in religion and their quest to know God. He used a statement from one of their own poets, "We are his offspring" (17:28), to seek common ground with their beliefs. He addressed the way God has made himself known. He stressed that God was not many but one and that God was clearly seen in Jesus Christ, whom God had raised from the dead (17:31). Because Paul used some of their own ideas, some of the philosophers wanted to hear more about the resurrection.

Churches have to be prepared to meet people where they are and to earn the right to witness. Our generation does not have the automatic entrée into people's lives as previous generations did.

The Conversion of the Masses

The straightforward witness of Paul and Silas to the gospel of Jesus Christ led the jailor in Acts 16:29–33 to conversion. In a moment in time he entered into eternal life with his confession of Jesus Christ. Not only was the jailor converted, but also his entire household was converted.

The use of the Old Testament Scriptures in witnessing in the synagogue in Thessalonica in Acts 17:1–4 led some Jews and a large number of "God-fearing Greeks," among whom were some prominent women, to be "persuaded" (17:4). The power of God's word used by the Holy Spirit convinced this group to accept Jesus as their personal Savior. Again, in Acts 17:12, Paul and Silas saw many Jews and prominent Greeks in Berea profess faith in Jesus Christ as a result of their searching the Scriptures.

A Christian does not need to try to outsmart a non-believer to convince that non-believer to be saved. The simple act of sharing the Scriptures unleashes God's power into that non-believer's life. Christians need to become familiar with the Scriptures so they can share with others on every occasion.

Perhaps one of the most difficult groups to convert was the philosophers Paul met on the Areopagus. However, we read in Acts 17:34 that a few people, including Dionysius, a member of the Areopagus; a woman named Damaris; "and a number of others" were converted. Paul met the philosophers and scholars where they were and introduced them to the good news of Jesus Christ. Paul used diverse methods to reach diverse people.

Our country is more diverse than it has ever been with so many different nationalities and religious beliefs. It is essential that Christians learn how to use diverse methods to share the gospel with these diverse groups.

Implications and Actions

The gospel is the power of God for salvation. That truth will never change. The method we use to share the gospel will change from person to person. Christians must become familiar with the gospel and trust the power of the gospel as they seek to share with the lost. We are not responsible for another person believing the gospel, but we are responsible to share that gospel.

QUESTIONS

1. In what ways did the conduct of Paul and Silas in the jail influence the jailor to want to be saved?

2. Why was it Paul's custom to go to a synagogue on the Sabbath?

3. Which group is harder to reach with the gospel—the religious or the pagan? Why?

4. How can churches share the gospel effectively with the growing number of people who do not grant authority to the Bible or the church as previous generations did?

NOTES

1. Unless otherwise indicated, all Scripture quotations in lessons 3–4, 6–8, 10–13 are taken from The Holy Bible, New International Version (North American Edition), copyright © 1973, 1978, 1984 by the International Bible Society.

FOCAL TEXT
Acts 28:17–31

BACKGROUND
Acts 21:17—28:31

MAIN IDEA
The conclusion of the
Book of Acts tells of Paul
turning to the Gentiles and
sharing the gospel without
hindrance in the capital city
of the Roman Empire.

QUESTION TO EXPLORE
What is hindering you
from sharing the gospel?

STUDY AIM
To decide that I will let
nothing hinder me from
sharing the gospel

QUICK READ
The Book of Acts ends with
the first-century fulfillment
of Jesus' command to be
his witnesses to the far
reaches of the world. Paul
did not let anything hinder
him from sharing the good
news with anyone who
was willing to listen.

LESSON THIRTEEN
Let Nothing Hinder You

I once went on a mission trip that included three delayed flights, two lost pieces of luggage, two unexpected hotel changes, one flat tire that took four hours to fix, one hospital emergency room visit, and one overnight stay at the airport. I cannot begin to describe the joy of finally arriving home and sleeping in my own bed! Have you ever been on a trip that didn't go the way you planned? Paul's trip to Rome certainly didn't. He got there, though, and he persisted in sharing the gospel anyway.[1]

ACTS 28:17–31

[17] Three days later he called together the leaders of the Jews. When they had assembled, Paul said to them: "My brothers, although I have done nothing against our people or against the customs of our ancestors, I was arrested in Jerusalem and handed over to the Romans. [18] They examined me and wanted to release me, because I was not guilty of any crime deserving death. [19] But when the Jews objected, I was compelled to appeal to Caesar— not that I had any charge to bring against my own people. [20] For this reason I have asked to see you and talk with you. It is because of the hope of Israel that I am bound with this chain."

[21] They replied, "We have not received any letters from Judea concerning you, and none of the brothers who have come from there has reported or said anything bad about you. [22] But we want to hear what your views are, for we know that people everywhere are talking against this sect."

[23] They arranged to meet Paul on a certain day, and came in even larger numbers to the place where he was staying. From morning till evening he explained and declared to them the kingdom of God and tried to convince them about Jesus from the Law of Moses and from the Prophets. [24] Some were convinced by what he said, but others would not believe. [25] They disagreed among themselves and began to leave after Paul had made this final statement: "The Holy Spirit spoke the truth to your forefathers when he said through Isaiah the prophet:

[26] "'Go to this people and say,
"You will be ever hearing but never understanding;
you will be ever seeing but never perceiving."

> ²⁷For this people's heart has become calloused;
>   they hardly hear with their ears,
>   and they have closed their eyes.
> Otherwise they might see with their eyes,
>   hear with their ears,
>   understand with their hearts
>   and turn, and I would heal them.'
> ²⁸"Therefore I want you to know that God's salvation has been sent to the Gentiles, and they will listen!"
> ³⁰For two whole years Paul stayed there in his own rented house and welcomed all who came to see him. ³¹Boldly and without hindrance he preached the kingdom of God and taught about the Lord Jesus Christ.

The End of a Long Journey

Paul finally arrived in Rome, although not the way he planned.² Paul had intended to travel to Jerusalem to deliver a financial offering that was to be a show of support to the Christians living there. The leaders in Jerusalem, however, did not welcome Paul as enthusiastically as he had hoped.

In Jerusalem Paul found himself embroiled in controversy. He was accused of bringing a Gentile into an area of the temple reserved for Jews only. Paul was arrested and spent the next two years in jail waiting for his legal case to be settled.

Paul was finally escorted to Rome in order to try his case before the Roman emperor. His journey to Rome was fraught with danger and setbacks. When Paul finally made it to Rome, a small contingency of Roman Christians walked eight miles south of the city to greet him (Acts 28:15). Christianity had already spread to Rome, most likely through the impact of Pentecost (2:10). In Paul's travels, he had come to know a group of Christians from Rome (Romans 16), and they had been anticipating his arrival. This surprise welcome must have lifted Paul's spirits. They led Paul into Rome, where he found temporary housing to await his appointment with the emperor.

Finally making it to your goal feels good. But Paul didn't let any grass grow under his feet. He didn't let the fact that he was still under arrest deter him. He didn't let the fact that he was in the largest and most influential city in the world intimidate him. He didn't let the fact that he had been rejected by his own people (the Jews) slow him down. Paul immediately began to share the message of Jesus Christ.

How often do you let the unhappy circumstances of life slow you down? Do you allow unexpected events to deter you from sharing Jesus? Things don't always go as planned. But we are still called to share the good news of God's love.

Paul's First Encounter with the Roman Jews

People appreciate a surprise ending to a good story. Acts provides just that in its closing verses. Bearing in mind what happened to Paul in Jerusalem, it stands to reason that the last thing Paul would want to do in Rome was connect with the Jews living there. And yet, unexpectedly, that was his first order of business.

PAUL'S NAME CHANGE

Paul's singular focus was on his mission to share Jesus. He was willing to do whatever it might take to accomplish his mission (1 Corinthians 9). Paul's name change is a good example. In the Greek world most people were given three names: a given name (*praenomen*), an original family or tribal name (*nomen*), and a particular family name (*cognomen*). Paul's particular family name was most likely *Paulos*. *Saulos* was probably his given name. We know that his tribal name, if he ever used it, might have been *Benjamin* (Philippians 3:5).

In any case, Paul changed his name usage from *Saul* to *Paul* on his first missionary journey when he traveled from the Aramaic-speaking world on Cyprus to the Greek-speaking world in Galatia. He had good reason to do so. In Greek *saulos* was used for someone who walked in a sexually suggestive manner like a prostitute.[3] Paul changed his name to remove any barrier to sharing the gospel message. What are you willing to change in order to better share Jesus?

Three days after the Christians welcomed him to Rome, Paul called a meeting with the Roman Jewish leadership (Acts 28:17). Luke summarized this encounter with a classic Greco-Roman rhetorical defense speech by Paul, a response by the Jewish leadership, and an agreement to continue the dialogue another day.

Paul's speech began with a brief address, followed by Paul telling his side of the story (in Greco-Roman rhetoric, a *narratio*), emphasizing his innocence and defending his actions. The *narratio* was followed by the *propositio*, that part of Greco-Roman rhetoric where the speaker proposes a solution to the problem, or a course of action.

Paul began by endearing himself to the Jews in Rome, calling them "my brothers" (28:17). He then proceeded to explain the circumstances that led him to Rome. He clearly stated that he had done nothing to violate the Jewish way of life, and neither had he transgressed any of the ancient laws of Judaism (28:17). He was wrongly arrested in Jerusalem and handed over to the Roman authorities.

Paul then described the process by which he was tried. The Roman authorities had examined Paul's case and found he was innocent of any crime deserving death. In Acts 24—26 Paul appeared before Felix, Festus, and Agrippa. All three cleared Paul of any wrongdoing. Agrippa concluded that Paul could have been released had he not already appealed to Caesar (26:32).

The outcry of the Jews in Jerusalem against Paul, coupled with the reported plot to assassinate him (23:12–22), had forced him to exercise his rights as a Roman citizen and appeal to Caesar (25:9–12). Paul quickly interjected that, although he had been falsely arrested, mistreated, and unjustly imprisoned for two years, he had no plans to file suit against the Jews in Jerusalem. As a Roman citizen, he had every right to bring a case against those who had mistreated him. Their case against him was weak. Paul had the testimony of three Roman rulers on his side. Yet, he was refusing to use his power as a Roman citizen to bring a counter-suit against the Jerusalem Jewish leaders (28:19).

Paul concluded with a proposition. He told the Jews in Rome that the reason he called them together was to let them know that, in spite of what they might have heard, he had nothing against the Jews and had no desire to harm them. He concluded that he found himself in trouble simply "because of the hope of Israel" (28:20).

APPLYING PAUL'S MESSAGE

Paul was in contention with the Jewish leaders because he was convinced that anyone who believed in Jesus was equally a child of Abraham. Read Galatians 3:28–29 and reflect on the following:

1. Why is the idea of this passage so radical?
2. In what ways do we violate the idea of this passage today?
3. What are some things that hinder people from coming to Christ?
4. What are some things you can do to cross racial, gender, and socio-economic class barriers in order to lead someone to Christ?
5. How might you inadvertently discriminate against someone, hindering the person from coming to Christ?

For Paul, the "hope of Israel" was obviously Jesus Christ. Paul concluded that it was because of what he was teaching about Jesus that he was threatened by the Jewish leadership in Jerusalem. Even some of the Jewish Christians were against him. What was Paul teaching that was so offensive?

Paul believed that Jesus Christ eradicated all differences between people (Galatians 3:28). The natural consequence of this was that it was permissible to have table fellowship between Jews and Gentiles. This was something that even the most devout Jewish Christians at Jerusalem were uncomfortable with (Acts 11:1–3; Gal. 2:11–14).

The other point of contention between Paul and the Jewish leadership was that Paul believed that the Christian community was the new Israel. This meant that the person who became a Christian was a child of Abraham (Rom. 4:16; 9:8; Gal. 3:7, 29). The idea that a Gentile could be a child of Abraham was unacceptable to the Jewish leadership in Jerusalem.

Paul's message would become the heart of the Christian movement. Salvation by faith in Christ apart from keeping the Old Testament law is foundational to our understanding of what it means to be a Christian. The belief that all people are created equal and deserve the opportunity to know God and to be an equal part of God's kingdom is so dear to us that it is difficult to imagine Christianity without it. Yet the church has always struggled to live out the truth of this belief.

The reaction from the Roman Jews was one of confusion and ignorance. They informed Paul that they had not received any letters from Jerusalem concerning him, and neither had they heard any bad reports from those arriving from Jerusalem (Acts 28:21). This must have been a great relief to Paul, for he seemed certain that news of his troubles had preceded him to Rome.

The Roman Jews also pleaded ignorance concerning the new "sect" that was forming around the person of Jesus Christ (28:22). They were interested in hearing Paul's views concerning this matter but felt that more people should be in on the discussion. So they agreed to a second meeting.

Paul's Second Encounter with the Roman Jews

After Paul's initial meeting with the Jewish leadership in Rome, an even larger group of Jews came to see Paul. This time the topic of conversation was the new sect of Judaism called Christianity. Paul had warned the Christians in Rome that he was eager to preach the gospel in Rome (Rom.1:15), and that when he arrived he would not be "ashamed" to preach the gospel of Jesus Christ (Rom. 1:16). Now he had his chance.

Paul used the Old Testament to try to convince the Jewish community that Jesus was the Messiah they had been waiting for (Acts 28:23). The reaction of the Jews was similar to the reaction Paul had received in other places. Some were convinced, others were skeptical, and others still were incredulous (28:24). The message that Paul preached had a way of dividing the Jews into two camps: the convinced and the angry. Typically this would lead to a heated argument, ending in physical confrontation (14:5; 14:19; 17:5; 28:24–25).

Paul ended the conversation by quoting "Isaiah the prophet" (Isaiah 6:9–10). Jesus had used the same line as he marveled at the disbelief of the people (Matt. 13:14; Mark 4:12). Paul then announced that although the Jews refused to believe, the gospel had been sent to the Gentiles, and they would embrace it. With that pronouncement the Jewish leadership, understandably upset, left Paul's residence. They were most likely shaking the dust off their feet as they left.

How do you feel when people reject your attempts to tell them about Jesus? Jesus called us to be his witnesses. Paul's life teaches us that we are not called to be successful. We are called only to be obedient.

Let Nothing Hinder You

Luke's narrative ends with a brief summary of Paul's circumstances in Rome (Acts 28:30–31). The legal charges against him must have been considered relatively mild. He was living under a very lenient form of confinement, best described as being under house arrest. He most likely had one Roman soldier guarding his residence but was free to move about the city within a certain parameter. He may have even been engaged in a tent-making business in order to pay the rent. He was also free to entertain as many guests as he pleased, whenever he pleased.

Under these circumstances, Paul boldly preached the good news of God's salvation and taught about the life and work of Jesus Christ. The city of Rome was considered the center of the known world. All the roads of the world truly seemed to lead to Rome. The narrative of Acts thus ends with the fulfillment of Jesus' words in the first chapter. The witness of the good news of Jesus Christ had, indeed, made its way from "Jerusalem, and in all Judea and Samaria, and to the ends of the earth" (1:8).

In spite of the unexpected twists and turns of life—the hills and valleys—God has a plan for your life. He will be faithful to fulfill his plan.

Implications and Actions

Paul endured countless trials and hardships in his quest to share Jesus with the world. He was verbally attacked, beaten, falsely arrested, shipwrecked, and bitten by a poisonous snake. Through it all he kept his focus on God's call for his life. He never wavered from the message that Jesus had given him to share. His radical idea that everyone who believed in Jesus was a child of Abraham and equal in God's sight made him plenty of enemies. Nonetheless, he never gave up on the task of sharing Jesus with a lost world. When the Jews rejected his message, he regrouped and found a willing audience in the Gentiles.

Paul teaches us the primacy of our call to share Jesus with others. He teaches us that God will always be faithful to help us, no matter what obstacles we face. He teaches us that we are not called to be successful in our mission, only obedient. Paul's example calls us to be faithful and obedient witnesses for Jesus in our neighborhood, city, state, and country, and to the uttermost parts of the earth.

QUESTIONS

1. Reflecting on Jesus' mandate in Acts 1:8, what is your Jerusalem, Judea, and Samaria? Can you name specific people in each?

2. What are some of the things that hinder you from sharing your faith?

3. How can you be a witness for Christ when things don't go the way you planned?

4. What are some of the circumstances in life that we sometimes use as an excuse for our lack of witnessing?

5. What are you willing to give up in order to be a better witness for Christ? What are you *not* willing to give up?

NOTES ───────────────────────────────────

1. Unless otherwise indicated, all Scripture quotations in lessons 3–4, 6–8, 10–13 are taken from The Holy Bible, New International Version (North American Edition), copyright © 1973, 1978, 1984 by the International Bible Society.

2. See Romans 1:15; 15:31–32.

3. Ben Witheringon, *The Paul Quest: the Renewed Quest for the Jew of Tarsus* (Downers Grove, Illinois: IVP Academic, 2001), 72.

Our Next New Study
(Available for use beginning December 2012)

THE GOSPEL OF MARK:
People Responding to Jesus

How to Order More Bible Study Materials

It's easy! Just fill in the following information. For additional Bible study materials available both in print and online, see www.baptistwaypress.org, or get a complete order form of available print materials—including Spanish materials—by calling 1-866-249-1799 or e-mailing baptistway@texasbaptists.org.

Title of item	Price	Quantity	Cost
This Issue:			
The Book of Acts: Time to Act on Acts 1:8—Study Guide (BWP001142)	$3.95	_____	_____
The Book of Acts: Time to Act on Acts 1:8—Large Print Study Guide (BWP001143)	$4.25	_____	_____
The Book of Acts: Time to Act on Acts 1:8—Teaching Guide (BWP001144)	$4.95	_____	_____
Additional Issues Available:			
Growing Together in Christ—Study Guide (BWP001036)	$3.25	_____	_____
Growing Together in Christ—Teaching Guide (BWP001038)	$3.75	_____	_____
Living Generously for Jesus' Sake—Study Guide (BWP001137)	$3.95	_____	_____
Living Generously for Jesus' Sake—Large Print Study Guide (BWP001138)	$4.25	_____	_____
Living Generously for Jesus' Sake—Teaching Guide (BWP001139)	$4.95	_____	_____
Living Faith in Daily Life—Study Guide (BWP001095)	$3.55	_____	_____
Living Faith in Daily Life—Large Print Study Guide (BWP001096)	$3.95	_____	_____
Living Faith in Daily Life—Teaching Guide (BWP001097)	$4.25	_____	_____
Participating in God's Mission—Study Guide (BWP001077)	$3.55	_____	_____
Participating in God's Mission—Large Print Study Guide (BWP001078)	$3.95	_____	_____
Participating in God's Mission—Teaching Guide (BWP001079)	$3.95	_____	_____
Profiles in Character—Study Guide (BWP001112)	$3.55	_____	_____
Profiles in Character—Large Print Study Guide (BWP001113)	$4.25	_____	_____
Profiles in Character—Teaching Guide (BWP001114)	$4.95	_____	_____
Genesis: People Relating to God—Study Guide (BWP001088)	$2.35	_____	_____
Genesis: People Relating to God—Large Print Study Guide (BWP001089)	$2.75	_____	_____
Genesis: People Relating to God—Teaching Guide (BWP001090)	$2.95	_____	_____
Genesis 12—50: Family Matters—Study Guide (BWP000034)	$1.95	_____	_____
Genesis 12—50: Family Matters—Teaching Guide (BWP000035)	$2.45	_____	_____
Leviticus, Numbers, Deuteronomy—Study Guide (BWP000053)	$2.35	_____	_____
Leviticus, Numbers, Deuteronomy—Large Print Study Guide (BWP000052)	$2.35	_____	_____
Leviticus, Numbers, Deuteronomy—Teaching Guide (BWP000054)	$2.95	_____	_____
1 and 2 Kings: Leaders and Followers—Study Guide (BWP001025)	$2.95	_____	_____
1 and 2 Kings: Leaders and Followers Large Print Study Guide (BWP001026)	$3.15	_____	_____
1 and 2 Kings: Leaders and Followers Teaching Guide (BWP001027)	$3.45	_____	_____
Ezra, Haggai, Zechariah, Nehemiah, Malachi—Study Guide (BWP001071)	$3.25	_____	_____
Ezra, Haggai, Zechariah, Nehemiah, Malachi—Large Print Study Guide (BWP001072)	$3.55	_____	_____
Ezra, Haggai, Zechariah, Nehemiah, Malachi—Teaching Guide (BWP001073)	$3.75	_____	_____
Job, Ecclesiastes, Habakkuk, Lamentations—Study Guide (BWP001016)	$2.75	_____	_____
Job, Ecclesiastes, Habakkuk, Lamentations—Large Print Study Guide (BWP001017)	$2.85	_____	_____
Job, Ecclesiastes, Habakkuk, Lamentations—Teaching Guide (BWP001018)	$3.25	_____	_____
Psalms and Proverbs—Study Guide (BWP001000)	$2.75	_____	_____
Psalms and Proverbs—Teaching Guide (BWP001002)	$3.25	_____	_____
Amos. Hosea, Isaiah, Micah: Calling for Justice, Mercy, and Faithfulness—Study Guide (BWP001132)	$3.95	_____	_____
Amos. Hosea, Isaiah, Micah: Calling for Justice, Mercy, and Faithfulness—Large Print Study Guide (BWP001133)	$4.25	_____	_____
Amos. Hosea, Isaiah, Micah: Calling for Justice, Mercy, and Faithfulness—Teaching Guide (BWP001134)	$4.95	_____	_____
The Gospel of Matthew: A Primer for Discipleship—Study Guide (BWP001127)	$3.95	_____	_____
The Gospel of Matthew: A Primer for Discipleship—Large Print Study Guide (BWP001128)	$4.25	_____	_____
The Gospel of Matthew: A Primer for Discipleship—Teaching Guide (BWP001129)	$4.95	_____	_____
Matthew: Hope in the Resurrected Christ—Study Guide (BWP001066)	$3.25	_____	_____
Matthew: Hope in the Resurrected Christ—Large Print Study Guide (BWP001067)	$3.55	_____	_____
Matthew: Hope in the Resurrected Christ—Teaching Guide (BWP001068)	$3.75	_____	_____
Mark: Jesus' Works and Words—Study Guide (BWP001022)	$2.95	_____	_____
Mark: Jesus' Works and Words—Large Print Study Guide (BWP001023)	$3.15	_____	_____
Mark:Jesus' Works and Words—Teaching Guide (BWP001024)	$3.45	_____	_____
Jesus in the Gospel of Mark—Study Guide (BWP000066)	$1.95	_____	_____
Jesus in the Gospel of Mark—Teaching Guide (BWP000067)	$2.45	_____	_____
Luke: Journeying to the Cross—Study Guide (BWP000057)	$2.35	_____	_____
Luke: Journeying to the Cross—Large Print Study Guide (BWP000056)	$2.35	_____	_____
Luke: Journeying to the Cross—Teaching Guide (BWP000058)	$2.95	_____	_____
The Gospel of John: Light Overcoming Darkness, Part One—Study Guide (BWP001104)	$3.55	_____	_____
The Gospel of John: Light Overcoming Darkness, Part One—Large Print Study Guide (BWP001105)	$3.95	_____	_____
The Gospel of John: Light Overcoming Darkness, Part One—Teaching Guide (BWP001106)	$4.50	_____	_____
The Gospel of John: Light Overcoming Darkness, Part Two—Study Guide (BWP001109)	$3.55	_____	_____
The Gospel of John: Light Overcoming Darkness, Part Two—Large Print Study Guide (BWP001110)	$3.95	_____	_____
The Gospel of John: Light Overcoming Darkness, Part Two—Teaching Guide (BWP001111)	$4.50	_____	_____
The Gospel of John: The Word Became Flesh—Study Guide (BWP001008)	$2.75	_____	_____
The Gospel of John: The Word Became Flesh—Large Print Study Guide (BWP001009)	$2.85	_____	_____
The Gospel of John: The Word Became Flesh—Teaching Guide (BWP001010)	$3.25	_____	_____

Acts: Toward Being a Missional Church—Study Guide (BWP001013)	$2.75	_____ _____
Acts: Toward Being a Missional Church—Large Print Study Guide (BWP001014)	$2.85	_____ _____
Acts: Toward Being a Missional Church—Teaching Guide (BWP001015)	$3.25	_____ _____
Romans: What God Is Up To—Study Guide (BWP001019)	$2.95	_____ _____
Romans: What God Is Up To—Large Print Study Guide (BWP001020)	$3.15	_____ _____
Romans: What God Is Up To—Teaching Guide (BWP001021)	$3.45	_____ _____
The Corinthian Letters—Study Guide (BWP001121)	$3.55	_____ _____
The Corinthian Letters—Large Print Study Guide (BWP001122)	$4.25	_____ _____
The Corinthian Letters—Teaching Guide (BWP001123)	$4.95	_____ _____
Galatians and 1&2 Thessalonians—Study Guide (BWP001080)	$3.55	_____ _____
Galatians and 1&2 Thessalonians—Large Print Study Guide (BWP001081)	$3.95	_____ _____
Galatians and 1&2 Thessalonians—Teaching Guide (BWP001082)	$3.95	_____ _____
1, 2 Timothy, Titus, Philemon—Study Guide (BWP000092)	$2.75	_____ _____
1, 2 Timothy, Titus, Philemon—Teaching Guide (BWP000093)	$3.25	_____ _____
Letters of James and John—Study Guide (BWP001101)	$3.55	_____ _____
Letters of James and John—Large Print Study Guide (BWP001102)	$3.95	_____ _____
Letters of James and John—Teaching Guide (BWP001103)	$4.25	_____ _____

Coming for use beginning December 2012

The Gospel of Mark: People Responding to Jesus—Study Guide (BWP001147)	$3.95	_____ _____
The Gospel of Mark: People Responding to Jesus—Large Print Study Guide (BWP001148)	$4.25	_____ _____
The Gospel of Mark: People Responding to Jesus—Teaching Guide (BWP001149)	$4.95	_____ _____

Cost of items (Order value) _____

Shipping charges (see chart*) _____

TOTAL _____

Standard (UPS/Mail) Shipping Charges*			
Order Value	Shipping charge**	Order Value	Shipping charge**
$.01—$9.99	$6.50	$160.00—$199.99	$24.00
$10.00—$19.99	$8.50	$200.00—$249.99	$28.00
$20.00—$39.99	$9.50	$250.00—$299.99	$30.00
$40.00—$59.99	$10.50	$300.00—$349.99	$34.00
$60.00—$79.99	$11.50	$350.00—$399.99	$42.00
$80.00—$99.99	$12.50	$400.00—$499.99	$50.00
$100.00—$129.99	$15.00	$500.00—$599.99	$60.00
$130.00—$159.99	$20.00	$600.00—$799.99	$72.00**

*Plus, applicable taxes for individuals and other taxable entities (not churches) within Texas will be added. Please call 1-866-249-1799 if the exact amount is needed prior to ordering.

**For order values $800.00 and above, please call 1-866-249-1799 or check www.baptistwaypress.org

Please allow three weeks for standard delivery. For express shipping service: Call 1-866-249-1799 for information on additional charges.

YOUR NAME _____ PHONE _____

YOUR CHURCH _____ DATE ORDERED _____

SHIPPING ADDRESS _____

CITY _____ STATE _____ ZIP CODE _____

E-MAIL _____

MAIL this form with your check for the total amount to
BAPTISTWAY PRESS, Baptist General Convention of Texas,
333 North Washington, Dallas, TX 75246-1798
(Make checks to "Baptist Executive Board.")

OR, **FAX** your order anytime to: 214-828-5376, and we will bill you.

OR, **CALL** your order toll-free: 1-866-249-1799
(M-Fri 8:30 a.m.-5:00 p.m. central time), and we will bill you.

OR, **E-MAIL** your order to our internet e-mail address:
baptistway@texasbaptists.org, and we will bill you.

OR, **ORDER ONLINE** at www.baptistwaypress.org.

We look forward to receiving your order! Thank you!